How to Build a Healthy Church

Crossway Books by Mark Dever

12 Challenges Churches Face

The Compelling Community: Where God's Power Makes a Church Attractive (coauthor)

Discipling: How to Help Others Follow Jesus

The Gospel and Personal Evangelism

How Can Our Church Find a Faithful Pastor?

How to Build a Healthy Church: A Practical Guide for Deliberate Leadership (coauthor)

In My Place Condemned He Stood: Celebrating the Glory of the Atonement (coauthor)

It Is Well: Expositions on Substitutionary Atonement (coauthor)

The Message of the New Testament: Promises Kept

The Message of the Old Testament: Promises Made

Nine Marks of a Healthy Church (4th edition)

Proclaiming a Cross-Centered Theology (coauthor)

The Unadjusted Gospel (coauthor)

What Does God Want of Us Anyway? A Quick Overview of the Whole Bible

What Is a Healthy Church?

Why Should I Join a Church?

"In the year 2000, I attended a weekender at Capitol Hill Baptist Church in Washington, DC. During our time there, Mark Dever allowed us to observe how they did church and invited us to ask questions. Everything the elders and the church did was intentional, and everything we observed was rooted in biblical convictions about what a church is and does. The Lord used that weekend to shape my understanding of what a healthy, biblical church might look like. What you hold in your hands is very much like a 'weekender' in book form. But make no mistake. This is not a 'how-to' book in the ordinary sense of that term. Instead, it is a 'why-to' book. In it, Dever and Paul Alexander argue that because the church is God's idea, we must order it according to his word. Our God determined church health, and he has revealed in his word how to pursue it. So read this book, consider what a church is, then deliberately lead your church toward that end for the glory of God."

Juan Sanchez, Assistant Professor of Christian Theology, The Southern Baptist Theological Seminary

"*How to Build a Healthy Church* is as simple as it is biblical. At the heart of the message is the presupposition that the Christian life is to be deliberately lived out in the community of a church family under the oversight of elders. Dever and Alexander provide no quick fixes, no new revelations; they simply call us to ordinary and consistent biblical Christianity."

Chopo Mwanza, Pastor, Faith Baptist Church Riverside, Kitwe, Zambia

"Here is one of the most faithful and insightful pastors of our time addressing the most crucial issues of church life. Mark Dever refuses to separate theology and congregational life, combining pastoral insight with clear biblical teaching. This book is a powerful antidote to the merely pragmatic approaches of our day—and a refutation to those who argue that theology just isn't practical."

R. Albert Mohler Jr., President, The Southern Baptist Theological Seminary

"This book is the perfect example of what a truly practical book on church health and growth should be: it gives concrete guidance for and examples of biblical principles being put into practice in the life and ministry of the local congregation."

J. Ligon Duncan III, Chancellor and CEO, Reformed Theological Seminary

"*How to Build a Healthy Church* shares many of the ministry lessons that Dever and his colleagues have learned from Scripture and sought to implement in the life of their church community. This book is for anyone who wants to get serious about following the biblical pattern for the church and is looking for down-to-earth practical help."

Philip Graham Ryken, President, Wheaton College

“Here is a novel idea: use the Bible as a handbook to gather and guide the church! And *How to Build a Healthy Church* is a novel volume indeed, standing amid the spate of ‘church-as-corporation, pastor-as-CEO’ manuals that glut church life. Here is a book that wafts a radical, refreshing breeze from the pages of Scripture that will breathe life into the church. A crucial read.”

R. Kent Hughes, Senior Pastor Emeritus, College Church, Wheaton, Illinois

How to Build a Healthy Church

A Practical Guide for Deliberate Leadership

Mark Dever and Paul Alexander

CROSSWAY®
WHEATON, ILLINOIS

How to Build a Healthy Church: A Practical Guide for Deliberate Leadership

Published by Crossway
1300 Crescent Street
Wheaton, Illinois 60187

Previous edition published in 2005 as *The Deliberate Church: Building Your Ministry on the Gospel.*

Cover image & design: Jordan Singer

First printing, 2021

Printed in the United States of America

All emphases in Scripture quotations have been added by the authors.

Trade paperback ISBN: 978-1-4335-7577-8
ePub ISBN: 978-1-4335-7580-8
PDF ISBN: 978-1-4335-7578-5
Mobipocket ISBN: 978-1-4335-7579-2

Library of Congress Cataloging-in-Publication Data

Names: Dever, Mark, author. | Alexander, Paul, 1973- author.
Title: How to build a healthy church: a practical guide for deliberate leadership / Mark Dever and Paul Alexander.
Description: Wheaton, Illinois: Crossway, [2021] | Includes bibliographical references and indexes.
Identifiers: LCCN 2020055535 (print) | LCCN 2020055536 (ebook) | ISBN 9781433575778 (trade paperback) | ISBN 9781433575785 (pdf) | ISBN 9781433575792 (mobi) | ISBN 9781433575808 (epub)
Subjects: LCSH: Church management. | Church work.
Classification: LCC BV652 .D455 2021 (print) | LCC BV652 (ebook) | DDC 254—dc23
LC record available at https://lccn.loc.gov/2020055535
LC ebook record available at https://lccn.loc.gov/2020

Crossway is a publishing ministry of Good News Publishers.

VP 29 28 27 26 25 24 23 22 21
14 13 12 11 10 9 8 7 6 5 4 3 2

To Connie and Laurie
Our partners in life, love, and ministry

Contents

Foreword

ONE OF THE STRANGEST DICHOTOMIES in contemporary evangelicalism contrasts theology with practical savvy. Many practitioners boast how little theology they know and amply demonstrate the warrant for their boast, while forcefully advocating a wide array of practical steps to foster church growth and discipleship. In response, many pastors and theologians bemoan the weightlessness of so much of contemporary evangelicalism and advocate a sober return to Scripture and a broad grasp of biblical theology. The former group often leaves the Bible behind, except in remarkably superficial ways: nothing challenges the hegemony of their methods. But the latter group, whose theology may be as orthodox as that of the apostle Paul, sometimes gives the impression that once you know a lot of the Bible and have read a lot of theology, everything will work out smilingly—as if there were no need for the practical advice of pastors who are no less committed to theology than they, but who are equally reflective on steps that must be taken, priorities, pastoral strategies, and the like.

A few years ago, Mark Dever gave us *Nine Marks of a Healthy Church* (soon to be in its fourth edition). Despite the feel of the title, this book was far removed from the kind of pop sociological analysis and managerial assessment with which we are often barraged. It was a book deeply embedded in biblical theology. Many pastors and churches have benefited from the faithfulness of its probing reflection. But suppose you live and serve in a local church that is far removed from the healthy profile developed in *Nine Marks*: What then? How do we get from here to there? Talking about those nine marks, and thinking through the biblical texts that warrant them, surely constitute part of the response. Nevertheless, the book you hold in your hands goes beyond that simplification to help pastors and other leaders guide a church toward spiritual health and growth. Once again, this book, jointly written by Mark Dever and Paul Alexander, is steeped in Scripture—but it is also chock-full of wisdom, years of pastoral experience, and godly insight. No pastor who is struggling "to get from here to there" should overlook this slender but invaluable volume.

D. A. Carson
Emeritus Professor of New Testament
Trinity Evangelical Divinity School

Mark's Preface

PAUL ALEXANDER REALLY WROTE THIS BOOK. We talked about the project for a while, and then, after some weeks, a few chapters turned up on my desk. Wow! I've not had quite this experience before. "Paul's written a book," I thought. "Why is my name on it?"

Then I started reading it, and I thought, "Hey, I've said that! That's how I put it! That's my story." And I realized what Paul had done. Paul took things that I've taught and written, things he's heard me say many times and questions he's heard me answer from visiting pastors, and he added his gifts of time, organization, clear writing and thinking ability—along with some of his own ministry experiences—and he produced the first draft of this book.

Paul and I had talked about all the things that should go in a book like this. We made sure that every question about the church that I seem to hear again and again was addressed—at least every question that we had anything helpful to say about. We worked together on the outline and the issues to be covered.

This book was actually my wife's idea. And it came about from her hearing the same questions asked again and again by visiting pastors, and me giving the same answers. I can't say that any wisdom represented in this book is particularly profound, but, by God's grace, it does seem to have been helpful to a number of ministers.

For the first edition of this book, we were initially thinking about calling it *Bodybuilding*, but there were simply too many debates among the staff members about who would be on the cover! So we settled for the title *The Deliberate Church*. We try to be intentional and thoughtful about what we do, because we realize that we are involved in the greatest task on earth—the building up of the body of Christ for his honor and glory. For this second edition, the publishers suggested a change in the title to make it more obviously related to *Nine Marks of a Healthy Church*, so we changed it to *How to Build a Healthy Church*.

If you've read other books that I've published about the church, you'll realize that this is the practical conclusion of a trilogy. The initial book, *Nine Marks of a Healthy Church*,[1] is my simple diagnosis of what ails great tracts of American evangelical churches today, along with the suggested biblical treatments. It is the most general and basic book. The middle phase of the project was the publication of *Polity*,[2] followed by some of its practical conclusions for modern churches in my book *Understanding Church Leadership*.[3] In these works I explored further issues of membership, discipline, and polity, and gave some practical applications. But it's in this present volume that Paul and I try to lay out some bottom-shelf "best practices" or "tips" for living out the ecclesiology represented in these other books. A theological synthesis can be found in my book *The Church: The Gospel Made Visible*.[4]

Special thanks go to my wife for suggesting this book, to Paul Alexander for putting so many hours in writing and cheerfully rewriting it, and to the good supporters of 9Marks for helping to make it possible. Paul is a talented and gifted writer. The elders and staff members here at the Capitol Hill Baptist Church have been wonderful teachers to me of much that we have shared with you in this book.

This book is meant to encourage you. We know we don't do everything correctly, and that some of our friends may be persuaded differently by Scripture on a few of the matters we're thinking about in this book, particularly church polity and the ordinances. On these matters, we simply invite you to consider the Word afresh with us and to be convinced in your own mind. We're always trying to learn from others as well. So by the time you read this, we may have already changed or modified some of the practices you see here. But we've found them helpful in living out the Bible's teaching about the church, and we hope that you may find them so as well. We hope we can instruct you, and even where we fail to instruct, we pray that we can provoke you so that you, too, will see your way to helping your church to live out the gospel more faithfully together.

It is to that end that all of us have labored, and it is to that end that I pray you will read and act.

Paul's Preface

MARK DEVER REALLY WROTE THIS BOOK. The words are mine, but they're mostly Mark's ideas; I've just put them on paper.

I first heard about Mark while I was doing graduate work at Trinity Evangelical Divinity School in Deerfield, Illinois, to prepare for the pastorate. I read his book, *Nine Marks of a Healthy Church*, for a pastoral duties class, and a professor of mine there, Mike Bullmore, encouraged me to take advantage of the internship program at Mark's church. I decided to think about his suggestion for a few weeks. When I had the rare occasion to call Dr. Bullmore at his home to clarify a detail, he asked me if I had gotten my application in for the internship at Capitol Hill Baptist. I said, "No, not quite yet." He responded with words I'll never forget: "Paul, pursue that with vigor." He didn't have to tell me twice. I turned in the application by the end of that week.

I met Mark for the first time in September of 2002 when I visited Capitol Hill Baptist on a 9Marks Weekender—a long weekend at the church that he serves in Washington, DC, designed to give pastors and seminary students a behind-the-scenes look at how a healthy church is led.[1] It only confirmed my desire to come and learn more. So I finished my classwork at Trinity that same semester and in January of 2003 started the internship program at CHBC.

It was more like an internship on steroids. My program at Trinity required four hundred hours of internship experience; the CHBC internship was eleven hundred-plus! I sat in on every elders' meeting; attended every corporate gathering of the church; read ten books on the church and wrote five response papers every week; met with Mark once a week for three hours with five other interns to discuss issues that touch the theology, leadership, and corporate life of the church; accompanied the pastors to almost every meeting they attended; and observed a model of evangelistic expository preaching that I had never seen. Those six months changed my life; they changed my understanding of what it means to be a pastor and to shepherd a church faithfully. It felt as if I had been catapulted twenty years ahead in my understanding of how biblical theology governs the life and leadership of the local church.

In God's kind providence, those months changed my life in another way, too: I met my lovely wife during those days—not surprisingly, a member of the church.

I stayed on with 9Marks as a contributing editor and continued attending the church, and God allowed me to soak even more deeply in the principles and practices that cultivate health and holiness in the local church. He also gave me the privilege of working shoulder to shoulder with a few good men, including Mark, the most faithful pastor I have ever met; and Matt Schmucker, the then director of 9Marks and the greatest boss and church administrator the world will ever know!

I'm deeply grateful to be a part of this project, and even more grateful for the opportunity to work with these brothers. They have been God's instruments in the continued formation of my personal character and pastoral understanding, and I know I would not be the man I am today without their patient instruction and faithful friendship.

The ideas represented in this book have reshaped my own understanding of what it means to be a faithful pastor. I pray they'll do the same for you, and that your church will become increasingly healthy as a result. *Soli Deo gloria.*

A Note to the Reader

WHY DID YOU TAKE THIS BOOK off the shelf? What caught your attention? Come on, be honest. Were you intrigued by the cover design? Did you read the endorsements on the back? Maybe you just picked it up because you like to stay current with the latest stuff out there on church growth and ministry models.

Or maybe the reason was deeper. Maybe you're a pastor who's been at it for a long time and you're discouraged by the lack of growth in your church. "What am I missing? Why am I not being as effective as the pastor down the road?" Maybe you picked it up because you're tired of not being "successful" in ministry—the fish aren't biting, so why not change the bait?

On the other hand, you might be a young-buck church planter who's looking to make an impact for the kingdom. Maybe you're tired of looking at a new world through old glasses and want to push the envelope—innovate, get creative, experiment with some new methods, try some crazy ideas, find out what really makes people tick in a post-everything generation.

Then again, maybe you've invested the last five years of your life trying to implement the latest church growth model and it didn't work. Maybe you're reading because you're disillusioned with the failure of a model that seemed promising and produced amazing results elsewhere. So now you're on to the next thing—what we call the *deliberate* church.

Maybe your interest was piqued by the possibility of a new way of doing church that might breathe fresh life into your congregation. Maybe you're reading it because it might be the next big wave in church ministry that could spark explosive growth in your church and light a fire in your community. Or perhaps you've just found yourself feeling a little outdated—a light blue leisure suit in a Bloomingdale's world—so you've come into the Christian bookstore to update the ministry wardrobe. Search your heart—why did you open this book? What are you looking for?

Before you start reading in earnest, let us clarify what this book is not, just for truth in advertising. First, *it's not new.* It's old—*really* old. We're not claiming that any of this stuff is original with us; it's not a "fresh take" or a "unique approach"—it's not innovative. In fact, we don't even *want* to be innovative (there, we said it!). Second, *it's not a program.* It's not something you can just plug into your church and press "Play." It's not dependent on technique; we don't have a set plan for spiritual maturity, or systematic steps for building a church; there's no flashy lingo or professional diagrams or cool metaphors. Third, *it's not a quick fix.* In other words, don't expect to read this book, implement its suggestions, and see immediate, observable results. Healthy growth takes time, prayer, hard work, patience, and perseverance.

"Well, if it's not a new program, then what is it?" Simply put, it's the Word building the church.

It's easy to agree with our culture that newer is invariably better. New clothes are better than old hand-me-downs; a new car is better than Dad's old beater. There is just something about new things that is almost irresistibly fascinating to us. They have this gravity that pulls us in with their glimmering shine, their new-car smell, their modern look, their promise of increased efficiency and effectiveness. We know it's dumb, but somehow they make us feel new with them—almost like we're renewed in their image.

When it comes to ideas on how to build the church, it's tempting to allow our fascination with the new to drive our thinking and determine our methods. This temptation is all the more seductive in the context of an emerging evangelical culture that increasingly distances itself from the clear proclamation of doctrinal certainties grounded in scriptural truth and handed down to us by the historic Christian creeds and confessions. As we are uprooted from our rich doctrinal and historical heritage, the innovative and creative begin to appear more plausible than the tried and true, in part because we are immersed in a culture that stridently embraces its own superiority to whatever is past. Pragmatism then naturally prevails. Without even realizing or reflecting on it, we quickly become excited about the most recent creative model that promises the most immediately observable results, usually measured by sanctified statistics.

At the root of all this, often unwittingly, is the rapid erosion of our faith in the sufficiency of Scripture for our effectiveness in ministry. Paul instructs Timothy to devote himself to preaching the Word (2 Tim. 4:2) precisely because that Word makes the man of God "adequate, equipped for every good work" (3:17). Timothy didn't need the latest rhetorical techniques, business practices, or creative ministry models based on captivating metaphors. He simply needed to be guided, governed, and geared by the Word of God.

Deliberate, of course, means well thought through or careful. What we are trying to be careful about as church leaders, then, is building the church on and around the gospel of Christ. More specifically, we are trying to be careful about building our church according to the pattern that God has given us in Scripture. At its best, the deliberate church is careful to trust the Word of God, wielded by Jesus Christ, to do the work of building the local church. It is an attempt to put our money where our mouth is when we say that we believe in the sufficiency of Scripture for the life, health, and growth of the local church. Our goal isn't to see how innovative we can be. Our goal is to see how faithful we can be.

What follows, then, *could* be called a model of ministry. But it's really just an attempt to be deliberate about treating the biblical gospel as that which feeds the church's growth, drives its progress, and governs every aspect of the church's corporate life and leadership. In whatever we do, we want to be careful about allowing God's Word to set our trajectory, power our progress, and govern our methods. From our preaching and evangelism, to the way we take in new members; from our discipleship and discipline practices, to our leadership models; from the structure of our Sunday morning services, all the way down to the agenda at the elders' meeting, we want our procedures to reflect reliance on the biblical gospel, submission to its claims, and awareness of its implications for our corporate life together.

The words of God in Scripture are the building blocks of the church. As pastors and church leaders, then, our first priority is to make sure that the gospel enjoys functional centrality in the church. That is, we must make sure that the gospel governs the way the church functions. When the gospel enjoys functional centrality, the church gains traction in the culture, because the gospel is the power of God for salvation (Rom. 1:16; 1 Cor. 1:17–18). The gospel is what gives people new spiritual birth (James 1:18; 1 Pet. 1:23). The gospel fights the church's enemies, such as doctrinal error and moral wickedness (Acts 6:7; 12:24; 19:20). In short, God's Word, encapsulated in the gospel, builds the church.[1]

Preserving this functional centrality of the gospel is the reason we don't want to promote programs, steps, and innovative metaphors in this book. To preserve functional centrality for the gospel, human method has to remain plain, or else it will naturally supplant the gospel's rightful role. In this way, our method in building the church will function in much the same way as a preacher's style of communication. A preacher can be so flamboyant and animated that his own personality becomes more noticeable and affecting than the message he's trying to preach. Similarly, the methods of pastors and church leaders in building the local church can become so prominent that they begin to siphon for themselves the glory for the church's growth that rightly belongs to the gospel alone. Our goal as preachers and leaders is to keep our methods basic and plain so that the gospel is cast in bold relief against the backdrop of our own admitted weakness.

Think Tank

1. Does the gospel enjoy functional centrality in your church? Why or why not? Are there ways in which your current model of ministry might siphon off the glory of the gospel for itself? How so?

We called the first edition of this book *The Deliberate Church* because we wanted a title that might serve to throw us into the fray of the church methodology debates. American evangelicalism is now dripping with various kinds of churches: *the Emerging Church, the Purpose-Driven Church, the Connecting Church, the Disciple-Making Church*, a critical assessment called *the Market-Driven Church*, and almost any other kind of church you could possibly want. We thought keeping the format of "the ____ Church" for a title might get our foot in the door of the debate. *Deliberate* was the best word we could find to succinctly describe what we're talking about. But it's mainly a term that (hopefully) will get us in on the conversation so that we can hold up a way of doing things that actually has been recovered from centuries past—a church driven and governed by the gospel. Capitol Hill Baptist Church in Washington, DC, has been the laboratory for testing these ideas over the last ten years. What follows, then, are applications of these principles that have proven fruitful and encouraging in our context. They are not intended to be taken as either exhaustive or exclusive, but simply as an attempt to revive a warm conversation about how we feed, lead, and protect the flock of God.

And now the million-dollar question: Is it replicable? Can you do this with your church? Of course—but not because it's a plug-and-play program, and certainly not because of any brilliance of our own in coming up with a transferable model. It's replicable because it is scriptural and plain. No matter what size your church is, where you're located, or what kind of people you're ministering to, you can always be deliberate about being gospel driven and gospel governed in everything you do. It's not dependent on discovering the spiritual and cultural preferences of a target audience. You don't have to implement a synthetic curriculum, be an incredibly creative thinker, or even be the most charismatic leader. You just have to trust that Jesus will build his church by the agency of his Spirit and by the power of his gospel without buying the newest program or following the most popular trend.

But let us be clear. We're not promising immediate, observable results. *God* is sovereign. *He* determines our times and places, the length of our days, and the fruit of our labors. God the Father and the risen Son sovereignly decide when to pour out the Spirit in greater measure.[2] Your work in Christ's vineyard won't be fruitful simply because you read this book or even apply this model. We do think, because it displays a measure of faithfulness and obedience to God's normative Word, that you will be more likely to see lasting fruit. But no one comes to Christ unless the Father draws him, and no one obeys the gospel unless the Spirit gives him the gifts of understanding, repentance, and belief—and only God makes things grow.[3]

Many church leaders today are saying that the church will be catapulted into the future only when her methods catch up with the times. We're saying the exact opposite. In a sense, our goal is to take the church into the future by reminding her of who she was originally intended to be. We think the church will be catapulted into the future only when the most noticeable thing about her corporate life is that it is carefully governed and powerfully driven by God's age-old, time-tested Word.

Still interested? We hope so. After all, the function of the gospel in the life of the church should be at the very center of our lives as Christians, let alone as pastors and church leaders. If you get through the last chapter and reject the whole "model," at least be deliberate about it—know *why* you're rejecting it. But if you read through the whole thing and agree with it, then you have a stewardship on your hands. Don't just leave it to collect dust—be deliberate about applying it. Talk it through over meals with your fellow church leaders. Look around at your church meetings and leadership structures to see what would need to change in order for them to become more carefully governed and driven by the gospel. Teach people the biblical principles behind the practical methods, and intentionally cultivate unity around that teaching. Then take corporate action and lead for change together in a wise, patient, and winsome way.

Introduction

What Are We Building?

It would be patently stupid to start construction on a building without first knowing what kind of building we plan to construct. An apartment complex is different from an office complex, which is different still from a restaurant. They all have different blueprints, different kinds of rooms, different materials, uses, and shapes. So the process of building will be different, depending on what kind of structure we're planning to build.

The same goes for building a church. A church is not a Fortune 500 company. It's not simply another nonprofit organization, nor is it a social club. In fact, a healthy church is unlike any organization that man has ever devised, because man didn't devise it.

It only makes sense, then, for us to revisit God's Word to figure out what exactly he wants us to be building. Only then will we understand how to go about building it. Negligence here will result in both temporal and eternal futility. Temporally, a church is a spiritually heavy thing to build, and it is designed for heavy relational use. It requires the strongest materials, and those materials must be placed in the correct, load-bearing positions specified on the biblical blueprint so that structural integrity is built in. No matter how beautiful the facade, our structure will crumble if we build on a sandy foundation or with shoddy materials.

Eternally, our work will withstand the fire of the last day only if we build with the "gold, silver, precious stones" specified on the biblical blueprint (1 Cor. 3:12). Building without that blueprint will virtually guarantee that we will build with the cheaper and more abundant resources of "wood, hay, straw," all of which will burn in the end (vv. 13–15). Ignoring God's plan for the church and replacing it with your own will ensure the eternal futility of your work. Here at the outset, then, it is critical to reflect biblically on this foundational question: What is a local church?

Fundamentally, God intends the local church to be a corporate display of his glory and wisdom, both to unbelievers and to unseen spiritual powers (John 13:34–35; Eph. 3:10–11). More specifically, we are a corporate dwelling place for God's Spirit (Eph. 2:19–22; 1 Cor. 3:16–17), the organic body of Christ in which he magnifies his glory (Acts 9:4; 1 Cor. 12). The Greek word for church is *ekklēsia*, a gathering or congregating of people. The church is God's vehicle for displaying his glory to his creation.

The uniqueness of the church is her message—the gospel. The church is the only institution entrusted by God with the message of repentance of sins and belief in Jesus Christ for forgiveness. That gospel is visualized in the ordinances of baptism and the Lord's Supper, both instituted by Christ. The distinguishing marks of the church, then, are the right preaching of this gospel and the right administration of the biblical ordinances that dramatize it.

The structure we're building, then, is fundamentally God centered—it is a Godward structure, designed to display the glories of God's character and the truth of his gospel. It is also an outward-looking structure; but even in its outwardness it is God centered, since we look outward for the purpose of spreading God's character and gospel through all the nations—to gather more worshipers for him and thus magnify his glory.

Ours is a ministry of magnification—making God's glory appear to the eyes of the world as big as it really is by bringing it into closer view and sharper focus in the form of the local church. What we are building, then, is not simply another nonprofit organization or Christian company. We are building a corporate, organic structure that will accurately magnify God's glory and faithfully communicate his gospel.

Jesus is the one who is ultimately building his church (Matt. 16:18). But he has graciously allowed us to participate in the construction process, and it is therefore according to his biblical blueprint that we must build the structure and life of the church. What are *you* trying to build?

How Should We Build It?

How then do you go about building a healthy church? Countless answers have been offered from different quarters of evangelicalism. Some think it takes knowing your target audience and attracting them by meeting their needs.[1] Others propose that the key is to have a vibrant network of small groups, where "real community" can happen. Many advise that we need to jettison the "old" methods that worked fifty years ago and embrace new ones that work in our postmodern context.[2] Some advocate a return to religious symbols in worship to give people the sacred experience and connection with the past that they're looking for at church.[3] Others say the way forward is to sell our church buildings and start developing house churches.[4] Still others say we are free to do whatever works in our own local context, as long as it is ethical.

So how do we navigate the modern-method maze? Is there a compass we can use that will lead us out? Is there a way to rise above the underbrush of synthetic ministry models so that we can get a bird's-eye view of the way forward?

What these and many other ministry models assume is that method isn't really all that important to God. "If it brings people to church or helps them feel like they've really worshiped on Sunday, it must be a good thing, right?"

When it comes to building a people for his own name and glory, God cares how we go about participating in his redemptive purposes. As we'll see in chapter 1, the gospel itself is God's constructive power for building the body of Christ (Isa. 55:10–11; Rom. 1:16; 1 Pet. 1:23–25). The Word builds the church. Our power is not in having small groups, meeting the felt needs of our target audience, using the right evangelism program, having funny skits, providing plenteous parking, or targeting our ministries to postmoderns. Our power is in our unique message—the gospel (Greek, *euangelion*)—not in our innovations. As such, our primary method must be to clearly communicate that message as widely as possible. Biblically, that means that we must faithfully preach it (Greek, *euangelizø*), fearlessly calling for repentance and belief as the only saving responses (Mark 1:14–15).

So before we start talking about the nuts and bolts of building the church responsibly, let us be clear on the relationship between the gospel of Christ and the method of its ministers.

1. *Theology drives method.* Whether we realize it or not, our thinking on the gospel will shape the way we share it. Our theology of the good news will be brought to bear on how we build the church.

2. *God's methods determine ours.* The methods we use to plant and water in God's vineyard must be subservient to and in complete harmony with the working of God's growth method—the gospel, as faithfully preached by his servants. Working contrary to God's processes often means working contrary to his purposes.[5]

3. *The gospel both enables and informs our participation in God's purposes.* We are not even able to enter the kingdom of God, much less minister in it, unless his gospel first does its work in us; nor do we know how to minister in his kingdom unless his gospel first provides the parameters for doing so. As such, the gospel alone must both shape and evaluate any ministry method we use.

4. *Faithfulness to the gospel must be our measure of success, not results.* The power of God for spiritual life and genuine holiness is in the gospel. So fidelity is paramount, not innovation, and not immediately observable results. Simon the Magician drew a crowd—he even had them calling him the Power of God; but his power, motive, and message

were fraudulent (Acts 8:9–11). Our call is to fidelity as messengers. Only God causes real growth (1 Cor. 3:6–7), and he does so by the gospel (Rom. 10:14–17; Gal. 3:1–5).

This gospel, then, is that God is our holy Creator and righteous Judge. He created us to glorify him and enjoy him forever, but we have all sinned, both in Adam as our representative head and in our own individual actions (Rom. 5:12; 3:23). We therefore deserve death—spiritual separation from God in hell (6:23; Eph. 2:3)—and are in fact already spiritually stillborn, helpless in our sins (Ps. 51:5; Rom. 5:6–8; Eph. 2:1) and in need of God to impart spiritual life to us (Ezek. 37:1–14; John 3:3). But God sent his Son, Jesus Christ, fully God and fully man (Phil. 2:5–11), to die the death that we deserved, and he raised him up for our justification, proving that he was God's Son (Rom. 5:1; 1:4). If we would have Christ's perfect righteousness credited to us, and the penalty for our sins accounted to him, we must repent of our sins and believe in Jesus Christ for salvation (2 Cor. 5:21; Mark 1:14–15).

This gospel alone (Gal. 1:6–9) is the one we are commanded to preach (2 Tim. 4:2). This gospel alone contains the theology that must drive our ministry methods. This gospel alone is the one God uses to create a people for himself. This gospel alone both enables and informs our participation in God's redemptive purposes. Consequently, this gospel alone deserves to shape and evaluate both our methods and our ministries.

What Will It Cost to Build Like This?

It's easy to be faithful when you're seeing success; after all, success is what silences the skeptics. You might be motivated to imitate a ministry model like this one not just because it's biblical but because it has produced success elsewhere. Yet we've just said that visible results cannot be the metric by which we measure our ministries, which raises a disturbing question: What if the immediate results are not what you envisioned? What if, in a dark turn of God's providence, your faithfulness starts looking like what the world would call failure? What if, for all your faithfulness and patience, your leadership is still ignored, people are still leaving, the church still isn't adding new converts to its numbers, or the gospel is still generating more conflict in the church than you expected? What if that same problematic leader is still threatening and plotting to get you fired, precisely because you're following the counsel in this book?

Of course, even faithful leaders have room to grow, so there will probably be some soul searching. No pastor is without his sins. Even so, if numerical growth, or even gospel progress, remains elusive, don't get jaded and don't give up. The gospel is still the power of God to salvation, and it is still doing its work in you and in those around you. Jesus is still your High Priest, and he knows what it's like to be sinlessly faithful and yet end his earthly life with little to show for it. Jesus's best twelve guys—the dynamic dozen!—all abandoned him when the rubber met the road. One of them outright betrayed him, another repeatedly denied ever knowing him, and one actually ran away naked (Mark 14:50–52). Jesus died the death of a damned criminal.

Small wonder we overhear the suffering servant praying, "I have labored in vain; I have spent my strength for nothing and vanity; yet surely my right is with the Lord, and my recompense with my God" (Isa. 49:4 ESV). Jesus felt that, thought that, prayed that—and if you serve him, then maybe you will, too. In a similar way, the apostle Paul was treated as an enemy by some of the very churches he planted (Gal. 4:16), and at his first public defense, none of his converts showed up to support him—not one (2 Tim. 4:16). Yet none of us thinks of Jesus or Paul as failures, do we?

Now, don't get us wrong. We don't want you to lead in a way that initiates unnecessary conflict. Be wise as a serpent and gentle as a dove. Know your context and your congregation, and adapt accordingly. There's no virtue in suffering simply because you spoke before you listened (Prov. 18:13). Patience is a pastor's preservative. Still, just because you take all the counsel in this book doesn't necessarily mean you'll end up pastoring a thousand-member church in the heart of a cool city. That doesn't mean it's not working or that your ministry has failed! God uses all kinds of pastors in all kinds of places in churches of all sizes. Moreover, not every pastorate, and not even every local church, succeeds in the way we might want or expect. God never promises his servants a celebrity spotlight or what the world salutes as success.

Remember what God said to Baruch in Jeremiah 45:5? "Do you seek great things for yourself? Seek them not" (ESV). Baruch wanted to be known as the scribe who served the prophet who turned the moral tide in Israel so that the people would avoid the exile, return to God, and see the renewal of the kingdom—you can imagine worse ambitions—yet it wasn't to be. Similarly, Elijah thought his own showdown with the prophets of Baal might just be the great turning point for God's people, yet he was sorely disappointed in their response to his ministry.

Don't misunderstand—we're gospel optimists, and we want you to expect great things from God, too. Be strong and courageous! But the book in your hand is not a fast track to explosive numbers or evangelical stardom. Nor can it exempt you from the costs of the cross. If you commit to building a healthy church on the foundation of the gospel, then prepare yourself for a cross-shaped life and ministry, because the gospel is the gospel of the cross. You are taking up your cross and following Jesus. He who saves his life will lose it, but he who loses his life for Christ's sake and the gospel will find it. A call to ministry is a call to die—to self, to sin, to selfish ambition, to idolizing your own success, and to enhancing your own image. If you've never died like this in ministry, then chances are you're not doing it right.

But it is worth the cost, because here's the hope: the call to ministry is a call to the kind of death that always issues in resurrection—maybe not immediately, but eventually. There is no glory in the Christian life or ministry without suffering first—not even for Jesus himself (Phil. 2:5–11). But if we do suffer with him, then we will be glorified with him (Rom. 8:17). No one who dies with Christ and for his sake will ever be left in the grave. He always raises his people.

Take it on the word of an old apostle: there's a depth of fellowship with Christ even in the midst of the suffering, not to mention in the power of his resurrection (Phil. 3:10–11). To suffer with Christ is one of the great privileges of Christian ministry—it is indispensable to Christ-likeness, and it is one of the great keys to our own fruitfulness (John 12:24–26). Our death to self in ministry is part of what God uses to create life in others. We are "always carrying in the body the death of Jesus, so that the life of Jesus may also be manifested in our bodies. For we who live are always being given over to death for Jesus' sake, so that the life of Jesus also may be manifested in our mortal flesh. So death is at work in us, but life in you" (2 Cor. 4:10–12 ESV).

Christian, expect a cross, even multiple crosses, in Christian ministry. And then expect God to raise you from the dead, time and again. "Indeed we felt that we had received the sentence of death. But that was to make us rely not on ourselves but on God who raises the dead" (2 Cor. 1:9 ESV). Jesus reproduces his sufferings in us, to reproduce his resurrection in us, so that when others see us, they see the power of Christ crucified—and risen. This is what Peter was preparing the churches for in his first epistle—suffering, and only afterward, glory. Jesus died in shame to rise in glory (1 Pet. 1:18–21) so that we might die to sin and live to righteousness. And he suffered, leaving you an example, so that you might follow in his steps" (2:22–24). Those steps lead through the cross; but praise God, they don't end there.

Think Tank

1. What's driving your church—the content of the message or the uniqueness of the presentation?

2. Is your ministry method driven by biblical theology or by what works?

3. Do you measure success by results or by faithfulness to God's Word?

SECTION 1

GATHERING THE CHURCH

1

The Four P's

WHEN I[1] WAS INTERVIEWING WITH Capitol Hill Baptist Church before they called me to be their pastor, someone asked me if I had a program or plan to implement for growth. Perhaps to this person's surprise (and perhaps to yours, too!), I responded that I didn't really have any great plans or programs to implement. I was just armed with four P's—I would preach, pray, develop personal discipling relationships, and be patient.

Preaching

Maybe even more surprising to some, I said that I was happy to see every aspect of my public ministry fail if it needed to—except for the preaching of God's Word. Now what kind of a thing is that for a pastoral candidate to say to a church? What I wanted to get across was that there's only one thing that's biblically necessary for building the church, and that's the preached Word of God. Others could do every other duty, but only I was responsible and set apart by the congregation for the public teaching of God's Word. This would be the fountain of our spiritual life, both as individuals and as a congregation.

God's Word has always been his chosen instrument to create, convict, convert, and conform his people. From his very first announcement of the gospel in Genesis 3:15, to his initial word of promise to Abraham in Genesis 12:1–3, to his regulation of that promise by his Word in the Ten Commandments (Ex. 20), God gives life and health and holiness to his people through the agency of his Word. From the reforms under Josiah in 2 Kings 22–23, to the revival of God's work under Nehemiah and Ezra in Nehemiah 8–9, to that great vision of the valley of dry bones in Ezekiel 37:1–14, where God breathes the life of his Spirit into his dead people through the preaching of his Word, God always sends his Word when he wants to renew life in his people and assemble them for his glory. God works through the agency of his Word. He even says as much in Isaiah 55:10–11:

> For as the rain and the snow come down from heaven, and do not return there without watering the earth and making it bear and sprout, and furnishing seed to the sower and bread to the eater; so will My word be which goes forth from My mouth; it will not return to Me empty, without *accomplishing* what I desire, and without succeeding in the matter for which I sent it.

The New Testament witness to the primacy of God's Word in his method is just as conspicuous. "Man shall not live on bread alone, but on every word that proceeds out of the mouth of God" (Matt. 4:4). The Word sustains us. "In the beginning was the Word, and . . . in Him was life. . . . And the Word became flesh, and dwelt among us" (John 1:1, 4, 14). Jesus, the Word made flesh, is ultimate life incarnate. "The word of the Lord was growing mightily and prevailing" (Acts 19:20; cf. 6:7; 12:20–24). The Word grows and fights. "And now I commend you to . . . the word of his grace, which is able to build you up and to give you the inheritance among all those who are sanctified" (20:32). The Word is what builds us up and preserves us. "For I am not ashamed of the gospel, for it is the power of God for salvation to everyone who believes" (Rom. 1:16; cf. 1 Cor. 1:18). The gospel, God's clearest expression of his Word, is his effective power for salvation.[2] "So faith comes from hearing, and hearing by the word of Christ" (Rom. 10:17). God's Word is that which creates faith. "[W]hen you received the word of God which you heard from us, you accepted it not as the word of men, but for what it really is, the word of God, which also performs its work in you who believe" (1 Thess. 2:13). The Word performs God's work in believers. "For the word of God is living and active and sharper than any two-edged sword, and piercing as far as the division of soul and spirit, of both joints and marrow, and able to judge the thoughts and intentions of the heart" (Heb. 4:12). God's Word convicts. "In the exercise of His will he brought us forth by the word of truth" (James 1:18). God's Word gives us new birth. James advises a little later, "in humility receive the word implanted, which is able to save your souls" (v. 21). The Word saves us. Peter also claims regenerating power for God's Word: "You have been born again not of seed which is perishable, but imperishable, that is, through the living and enduring word of God. . . . And this is the word which was preached to you" (1 Pet. 1:23, 25).

There is creating, conforming, life-giving power in God's Word! The gospel is God's way of giving life to dead sinners—and to dead churches (Ezek. 37:1–14). He doesn't have another way. If we want to work for renewed life and health and holiness in our churches, then we must work for it according to God's revealed mode of operation. Otherwise we risk running in vain. God's Word is his supernatural power for accomplishing his supernatural work. That's why our eloquence, innovations, and programs are so much less important than we think; that's why we as pastors must give ourselves to preaching, not programs; and that's why we need to be teaching our congregations to value God's Word over programs. Preaching the content and intent of God's Word is what unleashes the power of God on the people of God, because God's power for building his people is in his Word, particularly as we find it in the gospel (Rom. 1:16). God's Word builds his church. So preaching his gospel is primary.[3]

Praying

Many men, especially in the global West, are addicted to work. It's understandable— productivity offers a cleaner high than any drug, and without the hangover. This can be equally (even especially) true for pastors, because we are rightly careful about not being lazy or unfruitful in ministry. We want to prove ourselves hard workers in the Lord's vineyard, so that we hear, "Well done, good and faithful servant." Prayer, though, doesn't always feel as productive to us as chaining ourselves to the computer, leading a board meeting, counseling a troubled member, reading a good book with an aspiring pastor, or getting out there and doing the work of an evangelist.

The overcorrection, then, is to neglect or shortchange supplication because we wrongly assume that prayer is somehow akin to procrastination—putting off the work. The truth is, prayer is a necessary part of the work. Prayer shows our dependence on God. It honors him as the source of all blessing, and it reminds us that converting individuals and growing churches are his works, not ours (1 Cor. 2:14–16; 3:6–7). Jesus reassures us that if we abide in him, and his words abide in us, we can ask anything according to his will and know that he will give it to us (John 15:10, 16). What a promise! I fear it is so familiar to many of us that we are in danger of hearing it as trite. Yet we must hear it as that which rouses us from our sleepy prayerlessness and drives us joyfully to our knees.

What then should we pray for as we begin to work for the health and holiness of the church? (1) What more appropriate prayers could a pastor pray for the church he serves than the prayers of Paul for the churches he planted (Eph. 1:15–23; 3:16–21; Phil. 1:9–11; Col. 1:9–12; 2 Thess. 1:11–12)? Allow these prayers to be a starting point for praying Scripture more broadly and consistently.[4] This is another way you can unleash the transforming power of the gospel on the lives of church members. (2) Pray that your preaching of the gospel would be faithful, accurate, and clear. (3) Pray for the increasing maturity of the congregation, that your local church would grow in corporate love, holiness, and sound doctrine, such that the testimony of the church in the community would be distinctively pure and attractive to unbelievers. (4) Pray for sinners to be converted and the church to be built up through your preaching of the gospel. (5) Pray for opportunities for yourself and other church members to do personal evangelism.

One of the most practical things you can do for your own personal prayer life, and for the prayer lives of other church members, is to assemble a church membership directory (with pictures, if possible) so that everyone in the church can be praying through it a page a day. Our church's membership directory has about twenty-seven people on a normal page. We also have sections for members in the area who are unable to attend and for members out of the area; one page for elders, deacons, deaconesses, officers, staff members, and interns; and sections that record the children of church members, supported seminarians, supported workers (like missionaries), and former staff members and interns. We usually encourage people to pray through the page number that corresponds to the current day of the month (e.g., June 1, page 1; June 2, page 2; etc.).

Model for your congregation faithfulness in praying through the directory in your own devotional times, and publicly encourage them to make praying through the directory a daily habit. Your prayers for people don't have to be long—just biblical. Perhaps choose one or two phrases from Scripture to pray for them, and then pray a meaningful sentence or two from what you know is going on in their lives at present. Get to know the sheep in your flock well so that you can pray for them more particularly. And for those you don't yet know well, simply pray for them what you see in your daily Bible reading. Modeling this kind of prayer for others, and encouraging the congregation to join you, can be a powerful influence for growth in the church. It encourages selflessness in people's individual prayer lives, and one of the most important benefits is that it helps to cultivate a corporate culture of prayer that will gradually come to characterize your church as people faithfully pray.

Think Tank

1. Why is the preaching of the gospel so important for the life of the church?

2. What three Bible passages will you memorize for the purpose of praying for your church?

Personal Discipling Relationships

One of the most biblical and valuable uses of your time as a pastor will be to cultivate personal discipling relationships, in which you regularly meet with a few people one-on-one to do them good spiritually. One idea is to invite people after the Sunday service to call you in order to set up a lunch appointment. Those who express interest by calling and having lunch will often be open to getting together again. As you get to know them, you might suggest a book for the two of you to read together and discuss on a weekly, every-other-week, or as-often-as-you-can basis. This often opens up other areas of the person's life for conversation, encouragement, correction, accountability, and prayer. Whether or not you tell these people that you are "discipling" them is immaterial. The goal is to get to know them and to love them in a distinctively Christian way by doing them good spiritually. Initiate personal care and concern for others.

This practice of personal discipling is helpful on a number of fronts. It is obviously a good thing for the person being discipled, because he is getting biblical encouragement and advice from someone who may be a little farther along, both in terms of life stages and in terms of his walk with God. So in this way, discipling can function as another channel through which the Word can flow into the hearts of the members and be worked out in the context of a personal fellowship. It's good for the one who disciples as well, whether you are a paid pastor or a nonstaff member, because it encourages you to think about discipling not as something that only super-Christians do, but as something that is part and parcel of your own discipleship to Christ. This is in large part why you as the pastor will be wise to publicly encourage members to get together for a meal during the week with older or younger members and have spiritual conversations over books on Christian theology and living. Members need to know that spiritual maturity is not simply about their quiet times, but about their love for other believers, and their concrete expressions of that love. A healthy by-product of nonstaff members discipling other members is that it promotes a growing culture of distinctively Christian community, in which people are loving one another not simply as the world loves, but as followers of Christ who are together seeking to understand and live out the implications of his Word for their lives. These kinds of relationships are conducive to both spiritual and numerical growth.

As a pastor, a healthy by-product of your personal discipling of other members is that it helps break down defensive resistance to your pastoral leadership. Change will always meet resistance. But as you open up your life to others, and as they begin to see that you are genuinely concerned for their spiritual welfare (1 Thess. 2:1–12), they will be more likely to see you as a caring friend, spiritual mentor, and godly leader, and less likely to misunderstand your gradual initiatives for biblical change as personal power grabs, self-centered ego trips, or overly critical negativism. Developing these kinds of relationships establishes their personal knowledge of you, which is helpful in nurturing personal trust of your character and motives, and in growing an appropriate level of confidence in your leadership among the congregation. It gradually breaks down the "we vs. him" barrier that sadly but often subtly stands between a wounded congregation and a new pastor, and is helpful in paving the way for biblical growth and change.

Patience

When I arrived at Capitol Hill Baptist, I waited three months before preaching my first Sunday morning sermon. I simply attended. I had asked for this time in conversations that were held before I arrived. When I explained my reasons, the church leaders agreed. It showed respect for the congregation, it gave me time to learn what the people were accustomed to, and it showed them that I wasn't in a hurry to change everything. I realize not all of us have the luxury of waiting three months to preach after our arrival; but if it's possible, I'd recommend it.

The best way to lose your place of influence as a pastor is to be in a hurry, forcing radical (even if biblical) change before people are ready to follow you and own it. It would be wise for many of us to lower our expectations and extend our time horizons. Accomplishing healthy change in churches for the glory of God and the clarity of the gospel does not happen in the first year after the new pastor arrives. God is working for eternity, and he has been working *from* eternity. He's not in a hurry, and we shouldn't be either. So it is wise to show care for the congregation and concern for the unity of the church by not running so far ahead of them that people start falling behind. Run at a pace that the congregation can keep.

Of course, there are some things you might need to change rather quickly. But as much as possible, do these things quietly and with an encouraging smile, not loudly and with a disapproving frown. We are indeed to "reprove, rebuke, exhort." But we are to do it "with great patience and instruction" (2 Tim. 4:2). Make sure the changes you want to implement are biblical (or at least prudent!); then patiently teach people about them from God's Word before you expect them to embrace the changes you're encouraging. This patient instruction is the biblical way to sow broad agreement with a biblical agenda among the flock of God. Once this broad agreement is sown, change is less likely to be divisive, and unity less prone to fracture. As you work for change, work also to extend genuine, Christian goodwill toward people. "The Lord's bond-servant must not be quarrelsome, but be kind to all, able to teach, patient when wronged, with gentleness correcting those who are in opposition, if perhaps God may grant them repentance leading to the knowledge of the truth" (2 Tim. 2:24–25). Make haste slowly—and kindly.

The key to displaying and actually having this kind of patience is to have a right perspective on time, eternity, and success.

1. *Time.* Most of us think only about five or ten years down the road (if that). But patience in the pastorate requires thinking in terms of twenty, thirty, forty, or even fifty years of ministry. This puts all our difficulties into perspective. In an interview with 9Marks, John MacArthur looked back over forty years of pastoral faithfulness in the same church, Grace Community Church in Sun Valley, California.[5] His fifth year of ministry saw tumult and division among the leadership. But he persevered over the long haul and now says he's seeing what happens when a pastor stays thirty-five years longer than he should have from a human perspective: exponential fruitfulness, and a culture of godly graciousness and joy. Are you in it with your congregation for the long haul—twenty, thirty, forty years—or are you figuring on "moving up the ladder" by taking a bigger church in five or ten years? Are you building a congregation or a career? Stay with them. Keep teaching. Keep modeling. Keep leading. Keep loving.

If you're a young, aspiring pastor who has yet to receive from a church an external call to preach, choose wisely. No one can predict the future or see all possible outcomes. But it may be less than wise to accept a call from a church or location that you couldn't imagine staying with longer than a few years. Go where you can envision contentedly putting down roots for the rest of your life, and commit.

2. *Eternity.* As pastors, one day we will all be held accountable by God for the way we led and fed his lambs (Heb. 13:17; James 3:1). All our ways are before him. He will know if we used the congregation simply to build a career. He will know if we left them prematurely for our own convenience and benefit. He will know if we drove his sheep too hard. Shepherd the flock in a way that you won't be ashamed of on the Day of Accounting. "Do your work heartily, as for the Lord rather than for men, knowing that from the Lord you will receive the reward of the inheritance. It is the Lord Christ whom you serve. For he who does wrong will receive the consequences of the wrong which he has done, and that without partiality" (Col. 3:23–25).

3. *Success.* If you define success in terms of size, your desire for numerical growth will probably outrun your patience with the congregation, and perhaps even your fidelity to biblical methods. Either your ministry among the people will be cut short (i.e., you'll be fired) or you will resort to methods that draw a crowd without preaching the true gospel. You will trip over the hurdle of your own ambition. But if you define success in terms of faithfulness, then you are in a position to persevere, because you are released from the demand of immediately observable results, freeing you for faithfulness to the gospel's message and methods, leaving numbers to the Lord. It seems ironic at first, but trading in size for faithfulness as the yardstick for success is often the path to legitimate numerical growth. God is happiest to entrust his flock to those shepherds who do things his way.

Our patience flourishes when we cultivate gratitude and contentment with where the Lord has placed us. So if you're in a smaller congregation and it's early on in your ministry, then enjoy the simplicity and sweetness of that smallness as long as it lasts. Don't let your idea of the perfect become the enemy of what's already good in the church you serve. Love the congregation as it is, not as you hope it will become. Refuse to compare your situation unfavorably with that of other ministers you know. And if possible, seek out a brotherhood of like-minded fellow pastors in your local area who can share your joys, speak into your sorrows, help you keep things in perspective, and encourage you along the way.

Confidence in the Christian ministry does not come from personal competence, charisma, or experience; nor does it come from having the right programs in place or jumping on the bandwagon of the latest ministry fad. It doesn't even come from having the "right" graduate degree. Much as it was for Joshua, our confidence is to be in the presence, power, and promises of God (Josh. 1:1–9). More specifically, confidence for becoming and being a pastor comes from depending on the power of the Spirit to make us adequate through the equipping ministry of Christ's Word. "Such confidence we have through Christ toward God. Not that we are adequate in ourselves to consider anything as coming from ourselves, but our adequacy is from God, who also made us adequate as servants of a new covenant, not of the letter but of the Spirit; for the letter kills, but the Spirit gives life" (2 Cor. 3:4–6). And how does the Spirit make us adequate? What instrument does he use? It's not a program. It's Christ's Word. "All Scripture is inspired by God and profitable for teaching, for reproof, for correction, for training in righteousness, [Why?] so that the man of God may be adequate, equipped for every good work" (2 Tim. 3:16–17; cf. Jer. 1:9; Ezek. 2:1–7; 3:1–11). The one thing necessary is the power of Christ's Word. That's why preaching and prayer will always be paramount—no matter what fad tops the charts. Stake your ministry on the power of the gospel (Rom. 1:16).

Think Tank

1. Pick one person in your church whom you could start getting together with for his spiritual good.

2. Pick a book, or even just a booklet, that you'd like to read and discuss with him.

3. Could your ideas of time, eternity, and success be cultivating a spirit of impatience with the congregation you serve? If so, how? How might those ideas need to be reformed?

2

Beginning the Work

BUILDING A LOCAL CHURCH can be a daunting prospect. We often want to ask with Paul, "Who is adequate for these things?" (2 Cor. 2:16). So where do we begin with such a Herculean task? Is there any other foundation than the gospel? "For no man can lay a foundation other than the one which is laid, which is Jesus Christ" (1 Cor. 3:11).

Clarifying the Gospel

Patience is a pastoral virtue. But the one thing you don't want to be slow about is preaching the gospel (1 Cor. 2:1–5; 2 Tim. 4:1–5). Many new pastors of old churches assume a rudimentary understanding of the gospel and the Christian life among the flock. But assumption on our part too often leads to presumption on theirs. That is, when we assume the gospel instead of clarifying it, people who profess Christianity but don't understand or obey the gospel are cordially allowed to presume their own conversion without examining themselves for evidence of it—which may amount to nothing more than a blissful damnation. Our ministries are ultimately about "ensur[ing] salvation both for yourself and for those who hear you" (1 Tim. 4:16). Believing the true gospel, and responding to it in repentance and belief, is the only way to be saved. The gospel and its required response, therefore, are the very last things we want to assume that people know—even if some of them insist otherwise. The human heart is astoundingly deceptive (Jer. 17:9), nominalism (being a Christian in name only) has spread in our churches like gangrene, and misunderstandings about the gospel abound among professing evangelicals, especially regarding its relationship to other religions and its implications for our everyday lives. People need to hear the gospel—whether they're professing Christians or not.

What you win them *with* is likely what you'll win them *to*. If you win them with the gospel, you'll win them to the gospel. If you win them with technique, programs, entertainment, and personal charisma, you might end up winning them to yourself and your methods (and you might not!), but it's likely that they won't be won to the gospel first and foremost. "For we do not preach ourselves but Christ Jesus as Lord, and ourselves as your bond-servants for Jesus' sake" (2 Cor. 4:5). The implication is that once you try to turn the corner from technique, program, or entertainment to the gospel, it's likely that you'll either lose them or they will be converted to you, not Christ. The gospel of Christ has never needed the gimmicks of man to effect conversion in the soul (Rom. 1:16; 1 Cor. 2:1–5).

So how do we begin positively? For starters, put yourself in the background and preach Christ crucified. Clarify what the true gospel is, what the required response is, and what it means to be a Christian. Make sure people know that God is our holy Creator and righteous Judge; that we have all sinned against him, offending his holy character, alienating ourselves from him, and exposing ourselves to his righteous anger; that he has sent Christ to die the death that we deserved for our sins; that Christ's death and resurrection is the only way to be reconciled to the one true God; and that we must respond to this good news by repenting of our sins and believing in the gospel if we would be forgiven by God, reconciled to him, and saved from the wrath to come. Make sure people know that they must persevere in a lifestyle of repentance and belief, displaying an increasingly loving and holy lifestyle that proves we are his disciples (John 15:8; cf. Matt. 7:15–23; 1 Thess. 3:12–13; 1 John 3:14; 4:8).

Let the content of the gospel do the work. This doesn't mean you have to be intentionally boring. But it does mean you have to be intentionally self-effacing. Illustrations from personal experience are often subtly self-serving. People love them because they tell them about you; but this is precisely what the true gospel minister wants to be careful about in the pulpit—not because he doesn't want to be "authentic," but because such illustrations usually attract more attention to ourselves than to the gospel. So use them sparingly, if at all, especially in the early years of your ministry, when we are all the more prone to the hubris of youth and the pride of popularity.

Since all Scripture is ultimately about Christ, you can preach the gospel as a natural outworking of any biblical text (Luke 24:25–27, 45–47).[1] But at the outset, it might be wise to let Jesus do the talking as much as possible—people usually won't disagree with him! Perhaps begin with an exposition of Mark or John. Let them hear Jesus saying the hard truths of the gospel. Present them as his words, not yours. If the people in the pews are really Christians, his words will have more pull with them than yours; and if they're not, his words will be more effective in penetrating their hearts than yours will. This is why the expositional form of preaching is so important, not only at the outset but as a steady diet for the congregation—it presents the point of the text as the point of the sermon, grounding the authority of the sermon in the authority of the Scripture.

Clarifying the gospel is so critical, especially at the beginning of a work, because you want to ensure, as much as externally possible, the purity of the church's membership (i.e., that all members are truly converted). The more your congregation is clear on the gospel, the less likely it is that either tepid nominalism or carnal divisiveness will find air to breathe—and the more likely it is that you will forge healthy and growing unity around the good news that distinguishes the church from the world.

But when the gospel is clarified, things begin to happen in people's hearts. Yes, encouragement happens—and so does conviction. If it's been a while since a congregation has heard preaching that convicts, then expect to be surprised by someone in the congregation who doesn't like that feeling (or perhaps doesn't understand it) and is not afraid to let you know it!

If and when that happens, remember 2 Tim. 2:24–26: "The Lord's servant must not be quarrelsome but kind to everyone, able to teach, patiently enduring evil, correcting his opponents with gentleness. God may perhaps grant them repentance leading to a knowledge of the truth, and they may come to their senses, and escape from the snare of the devil, after being captured by him to do his will" (ESV).

Those hard conversations are not to be resented or avoided. Nor are we to be defensive for ourselves in those moments. We're to shepherd the sheep (and the goats!) with a patient kindness that helps our hearers drop their own defensiveness so they can repent afresh at the gospel truth that we are working to reestablish.

Cultivating Trust

People have to trust you if they're going to follow you. This means that you will need to make it easy for people to trust you, and you will need to do this without manipulating them. God's sheep know his voice, and they can recognize the presence or absence of his voice in yours. Three of the most important ways you can cultivate trust in your leadership among the congregation are expositional preaching, personal relationships, and humility.

1. *Expositional preaching.* As people see you being faithful to clearly present the point of Scripture as the point of the sermon (i.e., as they see you preaching expositionally), it will help them trust that you are submitting yourself to the text and intention of the Bible. Your vision

for the church will more likely be biblical if you are preaching through Scripture expositionally. As a result, people will be more likely to see that you are setting a biblical course for them, and that you are being careful to follow Scripture as you lead them. The more clearly you present God's Word, the more likely God's people are to hear the Good Shepherd's voice in yours, and to follow you as you follow him.

2. *Personal relationships.* We are simply less likely to trust people until we have had an opportunity to know them, especially when choosing our leaders. We want to know them—their personalities, their motives, their goals, their struggles—the list could go on. Be knowable. One of the biggest mistakes pastors make is thinking that a false demand for "professional distance" precludes us from having friends in the church. You are a sheep, too—you need relationships just as much as anyone else does. That is the nature of the church—it is a godly web of mutually sanctifying familial relationships. Relate—have conversations after church; take people out to lunch during the week; exercise hospitality by inviting people to your home for a meal; take an interest in people, and be open to answering their questions about you; offer to read a book with a younger Christian man; offer to have someone accompany you for conversation as you run errands. Give people a relational context in which they can develop love and trust for you as a fellow Christian.

3. *Humility.* As you relate, do so in humility. Two of the most godly and disarming ways to display humility are accountability and correctability. Be accountable. Invite a few men to keep you accountable in the areas of sexual purity, ambition, or other issues that you struggle with particularly. Do this not simply because you want people to trust you, but because you know you are sinful and need other Christians to help you live a trustworthy lifestyle. And when you know you are in the wrong, admit it freely. Be correctable. The mere fact that we're leaders doesn't mean we're always right. In fact, leaders usually have more opportunities to do things wrongly! Get used to admitting that you're wrong. It's normal—even for pastors. The sooner you get used

to it, the more easily the church will see and trust your integrity. As an incentive, remember that the church you serve will reflect the weaknesses you model over time. An uncorrectable pastor breeds uncorrectable people. Do you really want to lead a congregational meeting with a bunch of uncorrectable members? Genuine humility breeds genuine trust and growing Christians.

Think Tank

1. Why is it wise to make sure at the outset that every church member knows the gospel?

2. What are three basic ways you can cultivate trust in your leadership among the congregation?

3. Can you think of other godly ways you can cultivate trust?

Cleaning the Rolls

Most local Rotary clubs will take a person's name off the membership roll if he fails to attend the meetings for an extended period of time. Yet many churches will allow a person to stay on the membership roll for years after he or she has stopped attending! Membership should mean more in the church than it does in a Rotary club. One of the best ways to reinforce this is to teach on why membership in the local church matters.[2] No one is saved by either church membership or attendance. But membership in the local church is a church's external, public affirmation that the member is continuing to give evidence of genuine Christian conversion.

Biblically, if a member shows prolonged negligence in gathering with God's people, how can he say he loves them? And if he doesn't love them, how can he say he loves God (cf. 1 John 4:20–21)? *Pastorally*, if a member who could attend continually neglects to meet with the people of God, church leaders simply are no longer in a position to externally witness the fruit of his life, and for that reason can no longer externally affirm his conversion by uninterrupted membership. *Evangelistically*, meaningless membership damages the corporate evangelistic witness of the church in the surrounding community. Members usually go AWOL to cover up more serious sin; but they are committing that sin as people who are still likely to be known by others in your community as members of your church! In other words, they are sinning in ways that make your church look hypocritical to the unbelievers in your community.

Most seriously of all, when we allow prolonged nonattenders to keep their names on the membership rolls, we actually help deceive them into thinking they are saved when their behavior is in fact calling their salvation into question. If membership is the church's public affirmation of a person's conversion, then to leave a nonattender on the rolls could very well be damningly deceptive. What's more, if you are the pastor of your local church, then God will hold you in some sense accountable for the spiritual well-being of every member of your church (Heb. 13:17). Do you really want to be held accountable for the spiritual well-being of a member whom you have not seen at church in four years—or worse, a member you've never even met? Everyone loses when we allow nonattendance to go unchecked. It doesn't serve you well, it doesn't serve the nonattender well, it doesn't serve the church's reputation well, and it doesn't serve God's reputation well. For all these reasons, it is wise to remove from the rolls those members who have shown prolonged negligence in meeting with God's people.

The litmus test that reveals whether or not your church needs to do this is the ratio between members and weekly attenders. If the church you are serving has a substantially higher number of members than weekly attenders, then many of your members are neglecting to show up on Sundays. We will discuss in detail later the practicalities of removing nonattending members. Suffice it to say now, if you have this problem, teach clearly and patiently on the biblical value of membership (see 1 Cor. 5 on the need to distinguish between God's people and the world), try to contact the negligent members in order to instruct them and to notify them of your intentions, and remove them from the rolls if they don't repent and return to the assembly of God's people. Cleaning the rolls is one way you can clarify for people what it means to be a Christian. It's a way of clarifying the implications of the gospel.

Conducting Reverse Membership Interviews

Another way to clarify the gospel is by conducting "reverse membership interviews."[3] When I first came to Capitol Hill Baptist Church, I committed myself to conducting membership interviews with every potential new member of the church. I did this primarily to fulfill my pastoral responsibility of ensuring that each person we take into membership understands the gospel, has repented from his or her sins, has believed in Jesus, and has lived differently from the world as a result. I also began conducting "reverse" membership interviews. That is, I not only interviewed *potential* members—I interviewed *current* members in the same way. I called them "reverse" not because they were exit interviews, but because I was going in reverse order back through a list of people who had joined the church. I started with those who had joined most recently before I came, and I am still working my way back up the list of members, in reverse chronological order. I did this in order to avoid assuming that current members had understood and responded to the gospel savingly. I also did it so that I would not be responsible for enabling current members to presume they are saved based solely on church membership, attendance, and activity. Last but not least, I did it simply in order to get to know members better, and to let them get to know me better.

In these interviews, I ask, among other things, for a brief testimony, and during that time try to listen for evidence of whether or not the person has been known by his or her friends and associates as a Christian. I also ask all members and potential members to state the gospel in sixty seconds or less, looking for a clear understanding of justification by faith alone and the requirements of repentance and belief. They don't have to use those exact words—I'm just looking for an understanding and application of the concepts.

Preaching is the best, most important way to clarify the gospel week after week. But it is not the only way, nor is it the only important way. The way we take members in (and see them out) can be a powerful reminder of what the gospel is and what implications it has for the way we live our lives. If you are a new pastor of a long-standing church, start conducting reverse membership interviews with the members who got there just before you did. This will give you as the pastor an idea of whether or not the gospel is understood by the people in the pews, and it will give you an opportunity to individually clarify the gospel for those who are unable to articulate it accurately. It will also tip you off to those in your congregation who may need more focused and basic discipling attention, and will probably alert you to members who are not actually converted. Even if you are a long-time pastor of the same church, if you have never conducted these kinds of interviews and wonder whether or not people really understand the gospel of Christ, it would be worth it to go back and do this remedial work. Such plain-spoken conversations can go a long way toward "ensuring the salvation . . . [of] those who hear you" (1 Tim. 4:16).

Think Tank

1. How does cleaning the membership rolls clarify the gospel?

2. Why is it a good idea to conduct reverse membership interviews with current members?

3

Doing Responsible Evangelism

BUILDINGS ARE BUILT ON FOUNDATIONS. Some of the most critical groundwork in building a healthy church happens in our evangelism. Both in what we say and how we say it, we're saying something about how we understand not only the gospel, but its implications for our lives. Looked at from the ground up, the way we understand the gospel will inform the way we do evangelism. The way we do evangelism will inform the way our hearers understand the gospel. The way our hearers understand the gospel will inform the way they live the gospel. The way our hearers live the gospel will have a direct bearing on the corporate witness of our churches in our communities. The corporate witness of our churches will in turn make our evangelism either easier or harder, depending on whether that witness is a help or a hindrance. And difficulty, or lack thereof, in evangelism will come to bear on our church-planting efforts, which brings us back to laying foundations.

Including Essentials

The most important aspect of evangelism is the evangel—the gospel, the good news. If we're not getting the evangel right according to the Word, then whatever we're doing, it can't be called evangel*ism*. So what are the essentials of evangelism? We can sum them up in four words: God, man, Christ, and response. *God* is our holy Creator and righteous Judge. He created us to glorify him and enjoy him forever (Gen. 2:7, 16–17; 18:25; Matt. 25:31–33). But *man*kind has rebelled against God by sinning against his holy character and law (Gen. 3:1–7). We've all participated in this sinful rebellion, both in Adam as our representative head and in our own individual actions (1 Kings 8:46; Rom. 3:23; 5:12, 19; Eph. 2:1–3). As a result, we have alienated ourselves from God and have exposed ourselves to his righteous wrath, which will banish us eternally to hell if we are not forgiven (Eph. 2:12; John 3:36; Rom. 1:18; Matt. 13:50). But God sent Jesus *Christ*, fully God and fully man, to die the death that we deserved for our sins—the righteous for the unrighteous—so that God might both punish our sin in Christ and forgive it in us (John 1:14; Rom. 3:21–26; 5:6–8; Eph. 2:4–6). The only saving *response* to this good news is repentance and belief (Matt. 3:2; 4:17; Mark 1:15; Luke 3:7–9; John 20:31). We must repent of our sins (turn from them and to God) and believe in Jesus Christ for forgiveness of our sins and reconciliation to God.

God, man, Christ, response. Remember—it's not evangelism without the evangel.

Extending Invitations

Every time we present the gospel, whether in a public church gathering on Sunday or in a private conversation during the week, we need to invite people to repent and believe in the gospel, if our presentation of the good news is to be complete. What good is the good news if I'm never told how I should respond to it or what I need to do about it? We need to invite people to repent and believe.

But when we invite them, we need to make sure that they cannot confuse any other response with the only saving response. The stakes are high here, because if we allow ambiguity on this point, then we're actually helping deceive people about their own spiritual state by encouraging them to be assured of their salvation when they may not have genuinely repented and believed at all. The two responses that seem to be most commonly confused with genuine repentance and belief today are praying a prayer with someone and coming forward at a church service.

Often Christians will share the gospel with an unbeliever and then encourage him to pray a written prayer. People may indeed repent and believe this way. But then the well-meaning evangelist will encourage the "new believer" that "if you prayed that prayer and sincerely meant it, then congratulations! You are now a child of God." Yet praying a prayer is never offered in Scripture as a ground of assurance, nor is sincerity. Jesus tells us not to look at prayers and sincerity for assurance, but at our actions—the fruit of our lives (Matt. 7:15–27; John 15:8; 2 Pet. 1:5–12). The New Testament tells us to look at the holiness of our conduct, the love we have for others, and the soundness of our doctrine as the key indicators of our assurance (1 Thess. 3:12–13; 1 John 4:8; Gal. 1:6–9; 5:22–25; 1 Tim. 6:3–5). What this means is that we shouldn't encourage people to feel assured in their salvation based simply on a prayer prayed, with no observable fruit of repentance in their lives.

The same is true of people who come forward after a sermon at church. Often a person will come forward after a sermon, indicate a "decision for Christ," and then be accepted into membership right on the spot! No confirming evidence of fruit is able to be discerned, yet it is assumed (often wrongly) that the person has genuinely repented and believed because he has expressed an abundance of emotion, walked an aisle, or prayed a sincere prayer.

The product of this kind of "no evidence required" assurance is that people are taught to look at a prayer prayed twenty years ago as the reason to think they are saved, with no thought of the contradiction between their lifestyle and profession *now.* We may be filling our churches with such false converts, who then sin in ways that call the corporate testimony of the local church into question. This is not the way to build a healthy church, and it can actually hinder our evangelistic work—both inside and outside the local congregation.

We need to realize that people can pray sincere prayers and walk aisles after sermons without ever genuinely repenting and trusting in Christ. They've been doing it for two thousand years. The writer to the Hebrews warns us that many people have had apparently genuine spiritual experiences that nevertheless are not "things that accompany salvation" (Heb. 6:4–9; cf. 2 Pet. 1:6–10), but that faith, hope, and love are more reliable guides (Heb. 6:9–12). The only external evidence that the Bible tells us to use in discerning whether or not a person is converted is the fruit of obedience (Matt. 7:15–27; John 15:8; James 2:14–26; 1 John 2:3).

We are wiser to discontinue ambiguous evangelistic practices rather than allow them to continue confusing people as to what constitutes a saving response to the gospel. Granted, allowing ambiguity may increase the numbers on our membership rolls. But it deceives unsaved people into thinking that they are saved—the cruelest hoax of all. It also wreaks havoc on the purity of our churches and their corporate testimonies, allowing into our membership many professing Christians who are later discovered not to be Christians at all because they eventually revert to lifestyles that simply cannot characterize a true Christian convert.

Whether you are starting a new church or reforming an old one, continue to call people to repentance and belief—in your conversation and in your preaching. New converts should make a public profession of that faith. And that is what *baptism* is for.

Think Tank

1. What are the four elements that every gospel presentation should include?

2. Why should we be concerned about how we encourage people to respond to the gospel?

3. How might invitations, or altar calls, introduce spiritual confusion in people's minds?

Avoiding Entertainment

Many American churches have used entertainment-based methods of evangelism—theotainment, as it has been called by some—in sharing the gospel with both adults and children. With adults, it often takes the form of surveying target audiences and creating an evangelistic service in which everything from the music to the sermon is geared toward making them feel comfortable—a "sit back and enjoy the show" approach. With children, it takes the form of youth groups or Sunday schools that spend most of their time thinking up fun activities that will sneak the gospel in through the back door.

Now there is no reason to argue against communicating the gospel in an understandable, creative, or even provocative way. But evangelism that takes the form of entertainment has some harmful side effects. Remember—what you win them with is likely what you'll win them to. If you win them with entertainment, they're likely to be won to the show rather than the message, which increases the likelihood of false conversions. But even if they're not won to the show, entertainment-based methods make repentance virtually impossible. We are not encouraged to forsake our sin by having our senses amused or our preferences coddled. The gospel is inherently and irreducibly confrontational. It cuts against our perceived righteousness and self-sufficiency, demanding that we forsake cherished sin and trust in someone else to justify us. Entertainment is therefore a problematic medium for communicating the gospel, because it nearly always obscures the most difficult aspects of it—the cost of repentance, the cross of discipleship, the narrowness of the way. Some will disagree, arguing that drama can give unbelievers a helpful visual image of the gospel. But we have already been given such visual images. They are the ordinances of baptism and the Lord's Supper, as well as the transformed lives of our Christian brothers and sisters.

This is certainly not to stifle all creativity in supplemental evangelistic outreaches. We want to encourage creativity in finding ways to share the gospel. It is, however, to caution us against a reliance on entertainment for "effectiveness" in evangelism, especially when that evangelism happens in our weekly gathering for public worship.

Churches are most healthy when the gospel is most clear; and the gospel is most clear when our evangelistic methods are most plain.

Avoiding Manipulation

Many well-intentioned pastors never mean to manipulate anyone into repenting and believing. But some of the methods we use in sharing the gospel can be subtly manipulative, whether we perceive them to be or not. Sometimes pastors use service music in ways that play on the emotions, especially quiet music during an invitation or a concluding prayer that draws out the listener's affections and misguidedly encourages a decision for Christ based on feelings. Conversely, some pastors use more exciting music that ends up working the crowd into an emotional frenzy of expressiveness that isn't always or necessarily godly. Other pastors apply social pressure for people to pray a prayer or walk an aisle by singing the same hymn verse over and over until someone finally cracks. A few even use aggressive conversational tactics to pressure people into praying a prayer.

We shouldn't want our gospel presentations or invitations to be finally molded by what we think will "close the deal." If they are, then they reveal that we think conversion is something we can orchestrate, which is the furthest thing from the truth. Instead of using all our powers to convict and change the sinner, while God stands back as a gentleman quietly waiting for the spiritual corpse, his declared spiritual enemy, to invite him into his heart, let's preach the gospel like gentlemen, trying to persuade but knowing that we can't convert. Then let's stand back while God uses all of his powers to convict, convert, and change the sinner. Then we'll see clearly just who has the power to call the dead to life.

Being God Centered

Some evangelism strategies seek to make the gospel attractive to unbelievers by fronting all the benefits of Christianity and saving the costs for later. They promise that you'll experience more satisfaction, less stress, a better sense of community, and an increased sense of meaning in life—and you'll be prepared for eternity to boot!—if you'll just make a decision for Christ right now. Perhaps all of these things are right around the corner for the listening unbeliever. Yet what does this kind of "benefit evangelism" do to the biblical gospel? It makes the gospel appear to be all about me and improving my lifestyle and making me happier. Now, granted, we are the beneficiaries and God is the benefactor. We're not the ones "doing God a favor" by becoming Christians. Yet the gospel is not ultimately about me. It is about God making his holiness and sovereign mercy known. It is about God's glory, and gathering worshipers for himself who will worship him in spirit and in truth. It is about God vindicating his holiness by punishing Christ for the sins of all those who repent and believe. It is about making a name for himself in the world by gathering a people and separating them to himself for the spread of his fame to the nations.

"Benefit evangelism" fills our churches with people who are taught to expect everything to go their way just because they became Christians. But Jesus promises persecution for following him, not worldly perks (John 15:18–16:4; cf. 2 Tim. 3:12). We want to build Christians and churches who persevere through hardship, who are willing to suffer, be persecuted, and even die for the gospel of Christ because they value God's glory more than the temporal benefits of conversion. We don't want people to become Christians because it will reduce their stress. We want them to become Christians because they know they need to repent of their sins, believe in Jesus Christ, and joyfully take up their crosses and follow him for the glory of God.

There are indeed wonderful benefits to the Christian life, but being God centered in our evangelism by focusing less on the temporal benefits and more on God's character and plan makes for more Christians ready to suffer, and more churches motivated by God's glory.

Training Members

Ideally, the pastor won't be the only one doing evangelism, at least not for long. But if our members are to become faithful and fruitful evangelists themselves, then it's up to their pastors to equip them for that work (Eph. 4:11–12).[1] As a pastor, one of the first ways you can equip members to become faithful evangelists is to model it for them in your own sermons. One of the ways we do this is by simply addressing unbelievers in the middle of the sermon. For example, we'll say something like, "If you're an unbeliever attending with us, we're glad you're here. I wonder how you're hearing all this . . . "; "Have you ever thought about how the point of this text applies to you?"; or "We want to be clear with you about what the Bible teaches on this point." Then we'll simply engage them for a minute or two with an implication or application from the text that addresses a weakness in their worldview, challenges them to take God and the gospel seriously, or presents them with the urgency of repentance, the hope of the gospel, or the compassion of Christ in the midst of a heartless world.

Another fruitful way to train members for evangelism can be to start an ongoing inductive Bible study in which you model basic skills of observing, interpreting, and applying the text. As you study the Bible inductively, you're giving your people practice at asking the right questions of any passage. In the process, people will not only become more conversant with Scripture, but also will learn to handle the Word better for themselves, both in their private study and in their evangelistic conversations. Over time, members will become more familiar with Scripture, more adept at gleaning truth and correcting error, and more confident in reading the Bible with non-Christians who have honest questions about it.

We can also train members to do evangelism by distributing faithful gospel tracts like Matthias Media's *Two Ways to Live* or Greg Gilbert's *What Is the Gospel?* One idea would be to start a Sunday school class for adults in which you use the time each week to teach through the tract and then model an evangelistic conversation based on the tract you're using. This does double duty by clarifying the gospel for members and giving them gospel language to use with unbelievers.

Extending hospitality to unbelieving visitors is one of the most underrated ways to encourage them to drop their defenses and become more open to gospel conversation. But here again, ideally the pastor won't be the only one extending all the hospitality. In fact, hospitality extended by members can often be more effective (and less threatening!) than if the pastor is the one extending the invitation. If a pastor or team of elders can preach and model hospitality toward unbelievers, then the congregation can pick up on that and begin creating a culture at church where it's normal for members to initiate welcoming conversations with the non-Christians who visit; to foster gospel-centered friendships with them; to open their homes for unbelievers to visit for lunch after the service; to invite them out for lunch; or to set up times during the week to get together for coffee and conversation over what they saw and heard at church. Think of how evangelistically fruitful it could be if your whole congregation had a mindset to extend hospitality toward unbelievers for the purposes of the gospel in their lives!

Think Tank

1. Are there elements in your church's evangelism that are more entertaining than informative?

2. Are there ways in which your church's evangelism strategy is more like a marketing strategy?

3. Could your church's evangelism method be perceived as emotionally manipulative?

4. If the answer to any of the above is yes, what might be a healthy way to pursue change?

4

Taking in New Members

SECURITY HAS BECOME SOMETHING of a preoccupation in our modern day. We create and purchase all sorts of devices to protect the entrance to our homes. We commonly create electronic passwords so that important information in our computers or bank accounts is not compromised. We keep tabs on our keys so that we don't lose access to our cars, houses, or offices, and so that dangerous people will not gain access to them through our negligence. Airport terminals crawl with multiple metal detectors, and myriad security personnel guard the gates where people board. Even in the clubs and societies we join, access is often restricted so that the reputation of the organization is not compromised by unqualified members.

Yet with all the concern we show for security in almost every other aspect of our lives, it is surprising how careless many Christians and even pastors have become about the spiritual security of the local church—the apple of God's eye. I don't mean that we simply leave the doors of the building unlocked when everyone goes home after the morning service. I mean that many churches often leave the front door of membership unlatched. Now usually the door is left ajar out of sincere love for those who want to come in out of the cold. But the password of the gospel is often not required, the key of sound doctrine seldom made necessary, the verifying signs of holiness and love left unexamined—and the purity of the church left open to compromise.

We are trying to figure out how to go about building a healthy church. The health of any local church hangs in large part on the prior question of whether its members are spiritually alive. Dead members spread the diseases that are decomposing their souls—all of which are gangrenous forms of unrepented sin. So what we are interested in here is preserving the regeneracy of local church membership, and thereby preserving the corporate testimony of the local church in the surrounding community. That is, we are asking this question: How do we ensure, as far as externally possible, that every person we accept into membership is truly converted?

Where Is Local Church Membership in the Bible?

Is the issue of membership in a local church addressed in the Bible? This is perhaps one of the most frequently asked questions about church membership. It may seem like a stretch to say that local church membership is a biblical concept—that is, until we actually start looking for it in the Bible. It's not as pronounced as the atonement or justification by faith. But the evidence is there, and it is consistent.[1]

The discipline case in 1 Corinthians 5 assumes public knowledge of who's in the church and who's not. "What business is it of mine to judge those outside the church? Are you not to judge those inside? God will judge those outside. 'Expel the wicked man from among you'" (vv. 12–13 NIV 1984). Expelling makes sense only in the context of visible belonging. When Paul tells the Corinthian church to admit the man back into fellowship, he tells them, "The punishment inflicted on him by the majority is sufficient for him" (2 Cor. 2:6 NIV 1984). "Majority" makes sense only in the context of a recognized whole.

We know that lists of widows were kept in the New Testament church (1 Tim. 5:9), and the Lord himself keeps a list of all members who will inherit eternal life (Phil. 4:3; Rev. 21:27). One of the first things God does after redeeming his people is count them. The whole purpose of the military census in Numbers 1 was to make a list of Israelite warriors that could be relied on in battle—they were counted *in* so that they could be counted *on*. It was a way of clarifying, "Who is going to be shoulder to shoulder with us?"

And God has always wanted a clear distinction to be made between the world and his holy people. Part of the purpose of the plagues in Exodus was "that you may know that the Lord makes a distinction between Egypt and Israel" (Ex. 11:7; cf. 8:23; 9:4). One of the main reasons for the elaborate system of animal sacrifice and moral regulation in the Old Testament was to distinguish God's people from the surrounding culture.

Church membership, then, is a means by which we demarcate the boundaries of the church. This is logically implied by the negative sanction of corrective church discipline. Corrective discipline assumes that it is important for a person himself to know that he is a member of the church. He can't be expected to submit to the church's discipline if he is unaware of his own membership in the church. It also assumes that other members need to know whether or not a person is a member. If he's being disciplined, then the other members need to know that is the case in order not to associate with him (1 Cor. 5:9–12; 2 Thess. 3:14–15). Further, corrective discipline assumes that it is important for those outside the church to know who the members of the church are, because one of the main motives for corrective discipline is the corporate testimony of the church in the unbelieving community.

Again, the evidence is not abundant. But it is clear, and it is consistent. At the very least, then, we may say that local church membership is a good and necessary implication of God's desire to keep a clear distinction between his own chosen people and the worldly system of rebellion that surrounds them. It was modeled in Corinth, and it is still necessary for the purifying exercise of corrective discipline.

The New Members' Class

One way to make sure that the people we accept into membership are truly converted is to hold a mandatory new members' class. At Capitol Hill Baptist, we require new members to attend six one-hour sessions offered each week during our Sunday school hour: "What Is Our Statement of Faith?" (What will we believe?); "What Is Our Church Covenant?" (How will we live?); "Why Join a Church?" (Why is church membership important, and what does it entail?); "What Is the History of CHBC?" (How are we connected to the stream of Christianity that has come before us?); "How Do We Think about Missions and Outreach?" (What are our denominational organs and distinctives?); and "Life Together" (How do we live together as a local church?).[2]

Now obviously not all of these classes are necessary for making sure a potential member is truly converted. The main purpose of the classes is to confirm awareness of our expectations on the part of potential members. But each class asks an important question, and the health and unity of the church will depend on all the members being able to give, substantially, the same answers and biblical rationale. This membership class establishes our corporate beliefs, commitments, identity, and ways of working together for the spread of the gospel to the nations. As such, it both protects the purity of the local church and works toward establishing unity among its members.

If you have multiple nonstaff leaders, then it might be best for you as the pastor to teach the statement of faith class (since you are the primary doctrinal teacher of the congregation) and consider having nonstaff elders or leaders teach the other classes. This will help the new members get acquainted with the elders/leaders, and it will give the elders more practice in teaching, as well as establish their authority among the congregation.[3]

The Church Covenant

As mentioned before, a church covenant answers the question, How do we commit to living together? The form of the covenant is the way we express our commitment. The content of the covenant is the way we understand our commitment. Our church here in Washington, DC, was founded with such a covenant, and the original still hangs framed in our main meeting hall, complete with the original signatures from 1878.

Requiring people to sign a church covenant lets them know that they will be expected not only to believe the statement of faith but to live it out. It also lets them know how they will be expected to live it out—namely, in clear ways that build up the corporate body and enhance the corporate testimony of the church in the community. Implementing a church covenant helps to correct the misperception that members can live in either isolated individualism or unrepented sin and still be members in good standing. It provides a biblical standard of behavior for members, notifying them of what it means to be a member of the local church and reminding them of the obligations that membership entails for our lifestyles and interactions with each other. Church covenants make membership meaningful because they clarify the spiritual and relational commitments that membership signifies. Clarifying the commitments of membership promotes the health of the local church because it keeps nominalism at bay and keeps us accountable to growing in real Christian piety. And the more we grow in true Christian holiness and love, the more evidence we have that we are indeed Christ's disciples (John 13:34–35; 15:8).

You can publicly encourage members to use the church covenant as an instrument of personal examination just prior to taking communion. It may even be advisable to read the covenant corporately before congregational business meetings to remind members of how they have committed to conduct themselves even when dealing with the business of the church.

The Membership Covenant of Capitol Hill Baptist Church

> Having, as we trust, been brought by Divine Grace to repent and believe in the Lord Jesus Christ and to give up ourselves to him, and having been baptized upon our profession of faith, in the name of

the Father and of the Son and of the Holy Spirit, we do now, relying on his gracious aid, solemnly and joyfully renew our covenant with each other.

We will work and pray for the unity of the Spirit in the bond of peace.

We will walk together in brotherly love, as becomes the members of a Christian Church; exercise an affectionate care and watchfulness over each other and faithfully admonish and entreat one another as occasion may require.

We will not forsake the assembling of ourselves together, nor neglect to pray for ourselves and others.

We will endeavor to bring up such as may at any time be under our care, in the nurture and admonition of the Lord, and by a pure and loving example to seek the salvation of our family and friends.

We will rejoice at each other's happiness and endeavor with tenderness and sympathy to bear each other's burdens and sorrows.

We will seek, by Divine aid, to live carefully in the world, denying ungodliness and worldly lusts, and remembering that, as we have been voluntarily buried by baptism and raised again from the symbolic grave, so there is on us a special obligation now to lead a new and holy life.

We will work together for the continuance of a faithful evangelical ministry in this church, as we sustain its worship, ordinances, discipline, and doctrines. We will contribute cheerfully and regularly to the support of the ministry, the expenses of the church, the relief of the poor, and the spread of the gospel through all nations.

We will, when we move from this place, as soon as possible, unite with some other church where we can carry out the spirit of this covenant and the principles of God's Word.

May the grace of the Lord Jesus Christ, and the love of God, and the fellowship of the Holy Spirit be with us all. Amen.

The Membership Interview

Once a person has completed the membership class and heard the doctrines, ideas, and practices described there, the next step is for the potential member to ask for a membership interview. Some people will learn things in the class that dampen their interest in the church and cause them to look elsewhere. For those who want to pursue membership further, the interview is just another small step of initiative that they have to take to prove they are serious about becoming members. Once a list of people is collected who have indicated interest in a membership interview, it is wise for a pastor (or an elder, if the church is large) to conduct an interview with each potential member individually. This is usually a thirty- to forty-five-minute interview, and part of the purpose is to gather simple data such as personal contact information and family status. But the primary purpose is to gather important spiritual information. Here are some things to look for.

1. *The gospel.* The most important question for the protection of the purity of the church is to ask them to explain the gospel, preferably in sixty seconds or less. This may be intimidating for some, but that's okay—it is better for them to stutter in front of you now than to stand speechless before the Lord on the last day (it will be better for you on that day as well, in view of the accounting you will give to God; see Heb. 13:17). Look for the basics—God, man, Christ, response—even if they don't use the exact vocabulary. If they leave anything out, graciously ask leading questions. If they are still unable to articulate it, say it for them, and ask them if they have repented of their sins and believed in the gospel. If they still seem shaky on their understanding (not just articulation) of the gospel after this conversation, encourage them to go through an evangelistic Bible study with a mature member before recommending them for membership.

2. *Church history.* Ask what their previous church was and why they left. Many people change churches because of substantial biblical

disagreements or significant geographical moves. But some change churches within the same area for bad reasons. If they are coming from a church within thirty minutes of yours, be especially sure to ask why they want to switch. Don't perpetuate the shuffling of sheep or someone's potentially irresponsible pattern of behavior simply because you want your church to get bigger. Also, encourage the person to get a letter of recommendation from the previous church so that it is clear between pastors which one actually has pastoral responsibility for this particular person.

3. *Baptism.* Are they baptized? What was the mode of their baptism? Are they willing to be baptized if they have yet to do so?

4. *Church discipline.* Have they ever been disciplined by a church? If so, ask why.

5. *Personal testimony.* Ask for their personal testimony. I usually ask about the home they were brought up in, when and how they were converted, and their lifestyle since then, looking particularly for evidences of repentance after conversion.

See the Appendix for a sample church membership interview form.

The Ministry of New Members

Often we are tempted to encourage new members to jump right in, find a ministry niche, and serve. But this is less than advisable. We don't always know what kind of teaching people have received in their previous church—sometimes they need to clean up misunderstandings of the gospel or the church. So we want to ensure that they understand both the gospel and the church biblically, and that they develop a track record of faithfulness in church attendance and gospel application before we give them formal or public entrée into the spiritual lives of other members. Many of us need to hear Paul again: "Do not lay hands upon anyone too hastily and thereby share responsibility for the sins of others; keep yourself free from sin" (1 Tim. 5:22).

The Margin of Error

At the end of the day, we simply have to admit that the wheat will grow with the tares (Matt. 13:24–43) until the Lord returns. But that fact doesn't give us license for pastoral irresponsibility in the way we take new members into our churches. We need to be faithful to do all we can to externally ensure that no unconverted person becomes a member of our local church. Perhaps it sounds unloving to question people's salvation when they ask to become members of our churches. But if membership is a local church's external affirmation of a person's spiritual conversion, then the most *un*loving thing we can do is mislead condemned people into thinking they are saved by conferring membership upon them too hastily. If we love people, and if we care about the corporate testimony of our local church, we will protect both by being careful about whom we accept into membership. Don't leave the front door unlatched.

Think Tank

1. Why might it be wise to hold mandatory new members' classes?

2. How can a church covenant contribute to the health of a local church?

3. How can membership interviews contribute to the health of a local church?

5

Doing Church Discipline

DISCIPLINE IS, ADMITTEDLY, not a happy word. It's a little like Brussels sprouts—we know we should like them, but it sure seems like an acquired taste. Whether it refers to the correction of another or the control of the self, discipline seems overly restrictive to us—outmoded in a freedom-sopped culture. But Scripture both models and commands us to exercise church discipline. And if we hope to build healthy churches, then we must be willing to do it.

Formative and Corrective

If we were to compare discipline in the body of Christ to discipline in the physical body, then formative discipline would be like eating right and exercising, whereas corrective discipline would be like surgery. Formative discipline is how the church gets in shape, stays in shape, and grows. So preaching, teaching, discipling, leading small-group Bible studies, and gathering for corporate worship are all examples of formative discipline. These activities shape the way we grow, and they strengthen us for work, both as individuals and as a church. They can help prevent serious risk of false teaching, public scandal, contentiousness, or a host of other spiritual maladies; and they can even make the local church look more attractive to those on the outside.

Corrective discipline is like surgery—it corrects something that's gone wrong in the body so that more serious injury doesn't result. Rebuke, admonition, and excommunication (removal from the church membership roll and prohibition of taking the Lord's Supper) are all examples of corrective discipline. They correct the more serious errors that members make in doctrine and lifestyle. This chapter will deal primarily with how to carry out corrective discipline.

Neglecting corrective discipline can be deadly for a church. No one likes the prospects of going under the knife. But sometimes it is the knife that saves your life. The prospect of corrective church discipline, especially when public, is seldom pleasant. But unrepented sin and those who continually cherish it are cancers that must be removed if the body is to enjoy health and engage in productive work. Most of us can think of at least one church whose corporate testimony has been tarnished by neglecting to properly discipline an unrepentant member who has sinned in a publicly scandalous way. Personal accountability relationships can go a long way toward preventing such tragedies; and removing an unrepentant member from the rolls can do much to recoup the losses we suffer.

The Preventative Function of Accountability Relationships

Here's the good news—corrective discipline doesn't have to be public! Actually, in a healthy church, private corrective discipline is happening all the time. People in the church sin. But growing Christians welcome other Christians into their lives for the purpose of confessing their sins to one another (James 5:16; 1 John 1:5–10). That is, in large part, how spiritual growth happens—by accepting biblical correction. You need to be modeling this kind of humble accountability as a pastor and encouraging it in other members.

Confessing our sins to one another makes us bring our sins out into the light, where they can be dealt with in the context of mutually sanctifying friendships in which people are strengthening each other through prayer, encouragement, and application of the Word. Sin needs darkness to grow—it needs isolation disguised as "privacy," and prideful self-sufficiency disguised as "strength." Once these conditions prevail, sin is watered with the acid of shame, which then makes darkness appear more attractive to the sinner than light. But when we walk in the light by confessing our sins, we realize that we are not alone in our struggles, and we open ourselves to the protective rebukes and loving corrections that function as pesticides to curb the destructive and enslaving potential of habitual sin.

Bringing our sin into the light by confessing it in the context of personal accountability friendships helps to prevent the sins we struggle with now from becoming scandalous later. The wise pastor will publicly encourage such accountability relationships, understanding them as biblical, preventative measures that decrease the likelihood and frequency of sins meriting the public discipline of the church. Churches grow when sin is nipped in the bud.

The Context

Not every sin gets nipped in the bud. Whether it be for prolonged nonattendance or publicly scandalous sin, we will likely have to deal with a case of public church discipline sometime in our ministries. But before discipline can be productive, there must be a context of both meaningful spiritual relationships and structurally sound leadership.

Healthy member relationships must be recovered *before* corrective discipline can be carried out realistically. Jesus said that all men will know we are his disciples if we love one another (John 13:34–35). And Paul said that the church is an integrated body, "joined and held together by every supporting ligament, grow[ing] and build[ing] itself up in love, as each part does its work" (Eph. 4:16 NIV 1984). Relationships are the ligaments that support the growth of the church. The church needs to be a web of meaningful spiritual relationships in which people are engaging each other in casual conversation, spiritual conversation, mutually encouraging and sanctifying discipling relationships, mutual accountability, and small groups.

This loving engagement in each other's spiritual lives must be normalized in a positive and formative way *before* corrective discipline can be sustained. Without this context of deeply interpenetrating spiritual relationships, corrective discipline will be like walking up to a child whom you see only once a month and spanking him in the street. It will likely be perceived as harsh, if not abusive, rather than the tough but responsible outworking of loving concern for another's spiritual good.

It's also important to have a preexisting structure of leadership that will not buckle under the pressures of the situation. This is one of the most practical reasons for developing a plurality of elders, and for being committed to nonstaff elders outnumbering staff elders. Carrying out public corrective discipline as the only pastor/elder is possible, but it may not be wise. To proceed with such a case as the lone pastor/elder is to risk creating an "us vs. him" mentality—the congregation against the paid pastor. From within that leadership structure, it is often difficult to avoid the perception (however false) that the pastor is acting in an authoritarian or unilateral way—and for that reason it may also be difficult to avoid getting fired!

But if you have a few biblically qualified, congregationally affirmed nonstaff elders who outnumber you yet support your leadership in the decision, then the members are more likely to trust that the decision has been filtered through the judgment of other trusted leaders besides yourself. Further, the motion to discipline would come not just from you as an individual, but from the elders as a unified group. From within this leadership structure, other elders can provide you with wisdom in what to say, how to speak, when to proceed, and when to be patient. Conversely, they can (quite frankly) prevent you from doing something stupid, or from doing the right thing in an unwise way. They can also help diffuse unjust criticism by absorbing it together with you, or even in your stead in private conversations that might happen in the weeks before the congregational meeting in which the discipline is initiated.

Think Tank

1. How can accountability relationships make corrective discipline a more realistic possibility?

2. Why establish a plurality of elders before attempting corrective discipline?

The Care List

Another way to prepare a congregation for a case of public corrective discipline is to develop a "care list" to be presented verbally at a congregational meeting. The care list is a list of members who need particular prayer or attention for any number of reasons, many of which may not be sinful at all. Being "on the care list" doesn't necessarily mean that a person is sinning unrepentantly. But one use of the care list is to make the congregation aware of the need to pray for any member who has sinned unrepentantly or scandalously, and to invite members to ask the pastors or elders privately about the situation. Make the person's name available verbally to church members in the congregational meeting prior to the one in which the discipline will be carried out. During that prior meeting, share why each person is on the care list, and encourage people to ask you or an elder privately about the situation before the next meeting. Giving members the opportunity to privately air questions can make a dramatic difference in the way a congregation reacts to a public case of corrective discipline. It often removes the shock factor associated with discipline.

Removing a Member from the Rolls

To help people understand what is happening in a public corrective discipline case, teach them beforehand to understand excommunication as the removal of a member from the membership rolls and, more fundamentally, the exclusion of the person from taking communion. Also, make sure that members know that they are to treat the disciplined member as an unbeliever, based on that person's unrepentant attitude and behavior. This doesn't mean that the person is not welcome to attend church. We definitely want such a person to attend the weekly preaching of the Word, just as we would want any unbeliever to do so. Nor does it mean we should not try to persuade the excommunicated person to repent. It does mean, however, that we as members are to avoid eating meals, "hanging out," or even casually chatting with such people in a way that would suggest they've done nothing wrong (see 1 Cor. 5:9–13).

In an elder-led, congregational context, the motion to remove a member from the rolls would normally come as a motion from the elders (although it could just as well come from the floor). Since, as a motion from the elders, it would be a motion from more than one member, it would not need to be seconded.[1] All that would remain would be for the congregation to vote. The percentage of votes needed to carry the motion would depend on how you have decided that issue in your constitution.

Think Tank

1. How might a care list contribute to the increased health of your own church?

2. Read Matthew 18:17; 2 Thessalonians 3:6–15; Titus 3:9–11. How should we treat disciplined members?

Conclusion

Gathering a church is hard work. It takes diligence, watchfulness, wisdom, and patience. Some in the congregation may not understand why you are doing things the way you are. Some might become impatient when immediate results are difficult to see or numerical growth takes longer than they expected. Some may be offended that you seem to be questioning people's salvation by clarifying the gospel so often. Others might actually leave the church because the inherent offensiveness of the gospel begins to make them uncomfortable or even angry. All of this is okay. These are often the signs of pastoral faithfulness in the early years of a work.

Keep *preaching*. Keep *praying*. Keep building *personal relationships*. Keep being *patient* when people forget, misunderstand, or wrong you (2 Tim. 2:24). Keep cultivating trust among them. Keep trusting that Jesus will build his church by the power of his Word. Lay the foundation with patient, biblical wisdom. It's worth it. Doing this work now will ensure the structural integrity of the house decades later—and it will save you a bundle in repairs.

But gathering a church is also eminently worthy and exciting work! Don't give up! Don't give in to doubt, disillusionment, or fear of man! Take a longer view. God's purposes for all of human history revolve around the local church as the visible, corporate manifestation of his Son, Jesus Christ! He has ordained that his most important objectives both here and in heaven be accomplished through the agency of the local church (Eph. 3:10–11)! He has promised that his church will not fail (Matt. 16:18)! His love for the church is so great that Paul has to pray for capacity just to comprehend its dimensions (Eph. 3:17–19)! The church is of cosmic importance to God—literally. And as pastors and church leaders, we are privileged to build up this church that God loves so much, as we ourselves obey the gospel and follow Christ (Eph. 4:11–16). Model godliness (1 Tim. 4:12–16). Be strong and courageous—God's presence, power, and promises are all with you (Josh. 1:1–8). "Be sober in all things, endure hardship, do the work of an evangelist, fulfill your ministry" (2 Tim. 4:5).

Recommended Reading for Section 1

ON BEING A PASTOR

Ascol, Tom, ed. *Dear Timothy: Letters on Pastoral Ministry* (Cape Coral, FL: Founders Press, 2004).

Bridges, Charles. *The Christian Ministry* (Carlisle, PA: Banner of Truth, reprint 2001).

Carson, D. A. *The Cross and Christian Ministry* (Grand Rapids, MI: Baker, 1993).

ON PREACHING

Chapell, Bryan. *Christ-Centered Preaching: Redeeming the Expository Sermon* (Grand Rapids, MI: Baker, 1994).

Dever, Mark, and Greg Gilbert. *Preach: Theology Meets Practice* (Nashville: B&H, 2012).

Goldsworthy, Graeme. *Preaching the Whole Bible as Christian Scripture: The Application of Biblical Theology to Expositional Preaching* (Grand Rapids, MI: Eerdmans, 2000).

Helm, David. *Expositional Preaching: How We Speak God's Word Today* (Wheaton, IL: Crossway, 2014).

Stott, John. *Between Two Worlds: The Art of Preaching in the Twentieth Century* (Grand Rapids, MI: Eerdmans, 1992).

ON PRAYER

Carson, D. A. *Praying with Paul*, 2nd ed. (Grand Rapids, MI: Baker Academic, 2014).

Onwuchekwa, John. *Prayer: How Praying Together Shapes the Church* (Wheaton, IL: Crossway, 2018).

ON THE GOSPEL

Gilbert, Greg. *What Is the Gospel?* (Wheaton, IL: Crossway, 2010).

MacArthur, John. *The Gospel according to Jesus* (Grand Rapids, MI: Zondervan, 1994).

Ortlund, Ray. *The Gospel: How the Church Portrays the Beauty of Christ* (Wheaton, IL: Crossway, 2014).

ON CONVERSION

Butterfield, Rosaria. *Openness Unhindered* (Pittsburgh: Crown and Covenant, 2015).

Gilbert, Greg. *Assured: Discover Grace, Let Go of Guilt, and Rest in Your Salvation* (Grand Rapids, MI: Baker, 2019).

Helm, Paul. *The Beginnings: Word and Spirit in Conversion* (Carlisle, PA: Banner of Truth, 1988).

Lawrence, Michael. *Conversion: How God Creates a People* (Wheaton, IL: Crossway, 2017).

McKinley, Mike. *Am I Really A Christian?* (Wheaton, IL: Crossway, 2011).

Peters, Justin. *Do Not Hinder Them: A Biblical Examination of Childhood Conversion* (Justin Peters Ministries, 2017).

Piper, John. *Finally Alive* (Fearn, Ross-shire, Scotland: Christian Focus, 2009).

Wells, David. *Turning to God* (Grand Rapids, MI: Baker, 2012).

ON EVANGELISM

Dever, Mark. *The Gospel & Personal Evangelism* (Wheaton, IL: Crossway, 2007).

Metzger, Will. *Tell the Truth*, 4th ed. (Downers Grove, IL: InterVarsity Press, 2012).

Murray, Iain. *Revival and Revivalism* (Carlisle, PA: Banner of Truth, 1994).

Packer, J. I. *Evangelism and the Sovereignty of God* (Downers Grove, IL: InterVarsity Press, 1991).

Stiles, Mack. *Evangelism: How the Whole Church Speaks of Jesus* (Wheaton, IL: Crossway, 2014).

ON PERSONAL DISCIPLING

Coleman, Robert. *The Master Plan of Evangelism* (Grand Rapids, MI: Revell, 1994).

Dever, Mark. *Discipling: How to Help Others Follow Jesus* (Wheaton, IL: Crossway, 2016).

Piper, John. *Don't Waste Your Life* (Wheaton, IL: Crossway, 2003).

Ryle, J. C. *Holiness* (Moscow, ID: Charles Nolan Publishers, 2001).

Ryle, J. C. *Thoughts for Young Men* (Carlisle, PA: Banner of Truth, 2015).

Tripp, Paul. *Instruments in the Redeemer's Hands* (Phillipsburg, NJ: P&R, 2002).

Tripp, Paul. *War of Words* (Phillipsburg, NJ: P&R, 2000).

Welch, Edward. *When People Are Big and God Is Small* (Phillipsburg, NJ: P&R, 1997).

ON CHURCH DISCIPLINE

Dever, Mark. *Nine Marks of a Healthy Church,* 3rd ed. (Wheaton, IL: Crossway, 2013).

Leeman, Jonathan. *Church Discipline: How the Church Protects the Name of Jesus* (Wheaton, IL: Crossway, 2012).

Leeman, Jonathan. *Understanding Church Discipline* (Nashville: B&H, 2016).

Whitney, Don. *Spiritual Disciplines within the Church* (Chicago: Moody, 1996).

Wills, Gregory A. *Democratic Religion* (New York: Oxford University Press, 1996).

ON CHURCH MEMBERSHIP

Anyabwile, Thabiti. *What Is a Healthy Church Member?* (Wheaton, IL: Crossway, 2008).

Dever, Mark. *Nine Marks of a Healthy Church*, 3rd ed. (Wheaton, IL: Crossway, 2013).

Dever, Mark, ed. *Polity: Biblical Arguments on How to Conduct Church Life* (Washington, DC: 9Marks Ministries, 2000).

Dever, Mark. "Regaining Meaningful Church Membership," in *Restoring Integrity in Baptist Churches* (Grand Rapids, MI: Kregel, 2008).

Dever, Mark. *What Is a Healthy Church?* (Wheaton, IL: Crossway, 2007).

Dever, Mark, and Jamie Dunlop. *The Compelling Community: Where God's Power Makes a Church Attractive* (Wheaton, IL: Crossway, 2015).

Leeman, Jonathan, *Church Membership* (Wheaton, IL: Crossway, 2012).

Leeman, Jonathan, *Understanding the Congregation's Authority* (Nashville: B&H, 2016).

SECTION 2

WHEN THE CHURCH GATHERS

6

Understanding the Regulative Principle

NOW THAT WE'VE GATHERED A CHURCH, what do we do when we get together each Sunday morning? How should we do it, and why that way? Does it even make sense to think about how we "should" do things in a corporate worship gathering? Doesn't the Bible give us more freedom than that? In this chapter, we'll think about the biblical reasons for allowing Scripture alone to evaluate and structure our corporate worship gatherings.

The Regulative Principle

Briefly, the Regulative Principle states that everything we do in a corporate worship gathering must be clearly warranted by Scripture. Clear warrant can either take the form of an explicit biblical command or a good and necessary implication of a biblical text.[1] The Regulative Principle has been applied more or less strictly over the centuries. Its point is that God tells us in his Word how we are to approach him in worship, and so it is our duty to search the Scriptures to see what God tells us to do in life and particularly in church.

It is helpful to begin with D. A. Carson's irenic note that "theologically rich and serious services from both camps often have more common *content* than either side usually acknowledges."[2] Carson goes on to observe that "there is no single passage in the New Testament that establishes a paradigm for corporate worship."[3] Agreed. Yet in leading God's people in corporate worship, we are in some sense binding their consciences to participate in each part of the service. That binding is only legitimate insofar as it has positive scriptural warrant, because Scripture alone is worthy to bind the conscience and function as the final rule for faith and practice. Not surprisingly, Scripture is replete with examples of God caring deeply about the "how's" of our corporate worship.[4]

Worship Is the Purpose of Redemption

Multiple times in Exodus 3–10, corporate worship is said to be the purpose of redemption (3:12, 18; 5:1, 3, 8; 7:16; 8:1, 20, 25–29; 9:1, 13; 10:3, 7–11, 24–27). If corporate worship is the goal of redemption, then it only makes sense that God would reveal to his redeemed people how he wants us to worship him when we gather. And this is exactly what we find God doing once his people get to Mount Sinai. Would God be so careless as to leave the outworking of his purpose in redemption to the imaginations of an idolatrous people (see Ex. 32)? No. In fact, God had promised in Exodus 3:12 that his commissioning of Moses would be verified when Israel worshiped God on the very mountain where he had appeared in the burning bush. God picked the place. God picked the time. And when Israel arrived at Sinai, God greeted his people in Exodus 20–40 by stipulating the terms and procedures on which their worship of him would be predicated. Corporate worship is too central to God's purpose in redemption for him to leave the specifics of it to the likes of us.

God Cares How People Worship in the Old Testament

Exodus 20:4. The second commandment makes it clear that God cares about *how* his people worship him, not just *that* they worship *only* him.

"You shall not make for yourself an idol, or any likeness of what is in heaven above or on the earth beneath or in the water under the earth." God is forbidding a certain form of worship, even though that form was directed at worshiping him.

Exodus 32:1–10. In making the golden calf, Israel was attempting to set up an alternative to the system of worship that God had just revealed to Moses in Exodus 25–30 (vv. 1–6). God's jealous and violent reaction indicates how seriously he takes both himself and his worship (vv. 7–10). We are not to worship him in just any way that seems right to us. We're to worship him on his terms, and in the way that he has revealed.[5]

Think Tank

1. Read 1 Corinthians 14. What do you observe here about the dynamics of corporate worship?

2. Read Leviticus 10:1–3. What was it that made God so angry, according to the text?

God Cares How People Worship in the New Testament

John 4:19–24. Jesus tells the woman at the well that Samaritan worship was inadequate because it was based on a view of God informed only by the Pentateuch, not the whole Old Testament ("You [Samaritans] worship what you do not know," v. 22). Their sincerity was necessary, but not sufficient. Their worship was inadequate because proper worship is a response to who God has revealed himself to be, and if worship is a response to revelation, then it must be according to that revelation.[6] Jesus goes on to point out that God is looking specifically for those who will worship him "in spirit and truth" (v. 24). In other words, they will worship God by the indwelling Spirit according to the self-revelation of God disclosed most fully in Jesus Christ. For us, too, sincerity is essential, but it is not enough. Worship is regulated by revelation.

1 Corinthians 14. In his instructions on corporate worship, Paul encourages prophecy over speaking in tongues (vv. 1–5). But if tongues are spoken, "two or three prophets should speak, and the others should weigh carefully what is said" (v. 29 NIV 1984). Yet how else could they weigh what is said in the assembly but by the scale of Scripture? Paul goes on to reason that "God is not a God of confusion, but of peace" (v. 33). God's revealed character has governing implications for how we worship him. What is even more striking is that Paul himself, by the apostolic authority vested in him by the Spirit, is regulating how many prophets can prophesy at one time by that same Spirit! In other words, the apostolic revelation given to Paul by the Spirit is regulating how even Spirit-inspired charismatic gifts are exercised in the corporate assembly. Corporate worship—even charismatic worship—is regulated by revelation.

Why Does God Care about How We Worship Him?

God gives two main reasons as to why he cares about our worship. First, God wants us to think of him as he really is, not simply as we imagine him. The way we worship God turns around to shape the way we view God. How we worship shapes our view of who we think we're worshiping. Let's return to the golden calf. Aaron and Israel were trying to worship the true God; they were just using a golden calf to do it. So why was God angry about that? The reason is that a golden calf, as valuable and virile a symbol as it is, cannot adequately represent the transcendence, self-sufficiency, wisdom, and mercy of the living God. God didn't want Israel thinking about him as if he were nothing more than a gold-plated bovine! Anything we use to represent God turns and shapes our view of him. But nothing represents God adequately except for his written Word in Scripture and his living Word, Christ Jesus. That same rationale applies to any worship method we might choose today. If we use an entertainment ethos and atmosphere to introduce, represent, or relate to God, that very ethos and atmosphere are teaching people something about the way God is in himself and in relation to us. It suggests that he exists for our use, when in fact we exist for his use.

Second, God cares about how we worship him because we become what we behold. One of God's main critiques of idol worship, whether in violation of the first or the second commandment, is that those idols are insensate—they have eyes and ears, but cannot see or hear (Ps. 115:4–7). But the static nature of our idols has a dynamic effect on those who worship: "Those who make them become like them; so do all who trust in them" (Ps. 115:8 ESV; cf. Ps. 135:15–18; Isa. 41:24; 44:9, 18). We ourselves are molded into the image of both what and how we worship. We look like what we look at.

But becoming what we worship is actually how it's supposed to work—when we worship the right God in the right way. "And we all with unveiled face, beholding the glory of the Lord, are being transformed into the same image from one degree of glory to another. For this comes from the Lord who is the Spirit" (2 Cor. 3:18 ESV). Where do we behold God's glory? In Scripture and in Christ Jesus. Christians and congregations are transformed into Jesus's likeness by looking at his glory as we find it in Scripture. The implication for our corporate worship services is that every element and form of our gathered worship should show people from Scripture God's glory in Christ so that we can all be transformed together into an ever more faithful reflection of that glory. So what does that principle look like when we apply it?

7

Applying the Regulative Principle

JESUS IS BUILDING HIS CHURCH, and he's doing it by the power of his own Word (Matt. 16:18; Rom. 1:16; 10:17). He also regulates the church's worship by that same Word, graciously informing us how we are to approach him. How then can we structure our Sunday morning worship gatherings in a way that reflects God's commitment to shaping the church by his Word?[1] Church leaders who have been committed to seeing the church reformed according to God's Word down through the ages have had a common method: read the Word, preach the Word, pray the Word, sing the Word, see the Word (in the ordinances).[2] Often referred to by theologians as the *elements* of corporate worship, these five basics are essential to the corporate life, health, and holiness of *any* local church.[3]

Read the Bible

"Until I come, give attention to the public reading of Scripture" (1 Tim. 4:13). Pastors are commanded by God to see to it that Scripture is regularly read in the public, assembled congregation. Scripture is powerful—even when the person reading it doesn't try to explain it (Jer. 23:29; 2 Tim. 3:16; Heb. 4:12)! Carving out time in our Sunday morning services to read Scripture aloud, without comment, every week makes a statement about the value we place on God's Word. It says we are eager to hear the Word of the Lord—we desire it. It acknowledges that the life and growth of our local churches depend on the power of God's Word, and that we really believe that "man does not live on bread alone, but on every word that comes from the mouth of God" (Matt. 4:4). It acknowledges our own weakness in that we continually need to be reminded of what God has said. It says we're willing to listen to God's Word, to sit under it in order to be instructed, assessed, and evaluated by it. It says we're willing to agree with its presentation of reality and with its estimation and judgment of us. It says we're willing to submit to its verdict and commands without qualification. Yet if the regular public reading of Scripture says all this, what are we saying if we neglect it?

If reading the Bible in our public services is this important, then how do we decide which parts to read? One of the best ways to decide is to begin with the passage to be preached—certainly read that one before you preach it! But we can maximize our time in God's Word together if we make regular time for another passage to simply be read, without comment, in the service. If you plan to preach a passage from the Old Testament, then you could have another member publicly read one from the New Testament that either quotes that Old Testament passage or deals with the same theme—or better yet, sees Jesus as the fulfillment of it. Conversely, if you plan to preach a passage from the New Testament, then you might consider whether that New Testament passage quotes an Old Testament text; or maybe there's an Old Testament narrative that illustrates the point of the New Testament passage you plan to preach.

For example, let's say you're preaching on John 1, where we're told that the Word of God became flesh and tabernacled among us, full of grace and truth. Why not read the end of Exodus 40, where God's glory fills the tabernacle, to make the connection that Jesus embodies the fullness of God's presence and glory in himself? Or it could work the other way—preach Exodus 40, and read John 1 to prepare the congregation for hearing a Christ-centered exposition of an Old Testament text.

Preach the Bible

"Preach the word; be ready in season and out of season; reprove, rebuke, exhort, with great patience and instruction" (2 Tim. 4:2). Pastors are commanded by God to preach Scripture regularly. The preaching of God's Word is God's ordained method for communicating the gospel to sinners (Rom. 10:14–17; cf. Acts 8:4). Pastoring is ultimately about ensuring salvation for ourselves and others (1 Tim. 4:13–16). But we cannot do that work without devoting ourselves to preaching and teaching. This is true because the gospel is what ensures salvation (Rom. 1:16). Cease preaching *that* gospel and you will compromise your responsibility in ensuring the salvation of the souls God has entrusted to you.

This is why a regular diet of specifically evangelistic expository preaching is crucial. We don't *just* need to preach a salvation message each week—people need meat, not just milk (Heb. 5:11–14). Nor do we need to present *only* the point of a passage each week, isolated from its gospel moorings (1 Cor. 2:1–5). Our churches need a consistent diet of sermons that present the gospel and its implications as the natural outworking of making the point of a biblical passage the point of each individual sermon. Jesus said that all Scripture is ultimately about him (Luke 24:27, 45–47). He has given us both the permission and the mandate to read the whole Bible with gospel-colored glasses—and then to preach the gospel as we preach the point of the passage, addressing both believers and unbelievers with its truth, power, and implications.

In Christ-centered, evangelistic exposition, we are preaching to accomplish multiple but complementary goals. First and foremost, we want to exalt Jesus as Savior and Lord. We want unbelievers to be able to hear our sermons and be saved. That means we preach for *conversion*. So we should include a brief summary of the gospel somewhere in every sermon, ideally arising organically from the topic, theme, and point of our preaching text. But we also preach for *maturity* in believers, to root them more firmly in the knowledge of God and to equip them for more effective service to him.

Pray the Bible

"First of all, then, I urge that entreaties and prayers, petitions and thanksgivings, be made on behalf of all men" (1 Tim. 2:1). This command is given at the beginning of a chapter that gives instruction on corporate worship and organization. Paul wanted these prayers to be staples in Timothy's leadership of regular corporate worship. Jesus quoted Isaiah as saying that "My house shall be called a house of prayer" (Matt. 21:13). Pastors are commanded by God to lead their congregations in public prayer. Everything that happens up front in church is part of the teaching ministry of the church. You are either teaching the members of your congregation how to pray biblically, teaching them how to pray poorly, or teaching them not to pray at all, simply by how much time you carve out in the service for prayer and how you fill that time.

Scripture teaches us how to pray. Praying God's Word back to him in the corporate assembly communicates that we want to approach him on his terms, not ours, and according to who he has revealed himself to be, not who we would prefer him to be. We would be wise to incorporate the ACTS pattern of prayer in our corporate worship services. Interspersed among songs, Scripture readings, and even corporate readings of historic Christian confessions,[4] we could have solemn, humble, and Scripture-saturated prayers of *adoration*, *confession*, *thanksgiving*, and *supplication*. The prayer of adoration or praise would focus on praising God for his attributes and perfections. The prayer of confession would be a corporate confession of the ways we have sinned against God since we last gathered, particularly focusing on ways we have disobeyed a publicly read passage of Scripture, the Ten Commandments, or the passage to be preached that morning.[5] The prayer of thanksgiving would focus on expressing gratitude for both spiritual and physical gifts that

God has given us. And the prayer of supplication would function as the pastoral prayer as the pastor brings the needs of the congregation before God, prays for public authorities, prays for the local church from the priorities of Paul's prayers for the churches, and possibly even prays the main points of the sermon for the congregation.[6]

Such prayers acknowledge our corporate dependence on God. They also serve people well not only in leading them in well-rounded corporate worship but in modeling for them maturity and reverence in approaching God in prayer. If you are pastorally frustrated that your church is not a praying church, ask yourself: Are they seeing it modeled?[7]

Sing the Bible

"Speak to one another with psalms, hymns, and spiritual songs. Sing and make music in your heart to the Lord" (Eph. 5:19 NIV 1984). The whole Ephesian church was commanded to build one another up and praise God through song. Part of pastoral leadership, then, is to facilitate this kind of edifying worship. But again, Jesus uses his Word to build or edify the church. So it makes sense that we only sing songs that use his Word both accurately and generously. The more accurately applied scriptural theology, phrases, and allusions, the better—because the Word builds the church, and music helps us remember that Word, which we seem so quickly to forget.

This certainly doesn't mean that you have to use hymns and older songs exclusively. There is actually much wisdom and edification in employing a variety of musical styles so that people's musical tastes broaden over time with wider exposure to different musical genres and time periods. This wider exposure can help curb the intensity of people's musical preferences based on personal tradition and experience, which in turn will lessen the likelihood of division or conflict over issues of musical style. Careful planning here can help defuse the most notorious bombs of the "worship wars."

It does mean, however, that you as the pastor must be theologically discerning in what you encourage and lead your congregation to sing. It also means you must show courage in not allowing yourself to be guided by the musical preferences of the culture or the congregation, or even the passion of a music director, but rather by the theological content of the songs and their edification potential. Edification—building people up—happens when people are encouraged to understand and apply the gospel more biblically, not necessarily when they are led into an emotional experience or encouraged to identify temporary emotional expressiveness with worship.

Lyrics set to music have formative power because they are memorable. Use songs that fill our minds with God's character, that form our worldview by God's truth, and that teach us about the biblical meaning and personal implications of his gospel. Just as with prayer, so here, everything that happens up front in corporate gatherings is a function of the teaching ministry of the church. As the main teaching pastor, it is therefore your responsibility to shepherd the congregation into the green pastures of God-centered, gospel-centered songs, and away from the arid plains of theological vacuity, meditations on human experience, and emotional frenzy. The best of the hymns and the best of the more modern worship choruses are those that direct our focus away from ourselves and onto the character and gospel of God.[9] Practice discerning the difference, and be careful about what you're teaching through the music you encourage people to sing. If at all possible, refuse to pawn this responsibility off to someone else. God will hold us accountable for this aspect of our teaching ministries as well—even if we do delegate it (Heb. 13:17).

Think Tank

1. Why is the pastor responsible for the music that's sung in the church?

2. Are there songs in your church's repertoire that teach your congregation poorly?

See the Bible

"Do this in remembrance of Me" (Luke 22:19). The ordinances are the dramatic presentations of the gospel. They are the moving pictures that represent the spiritual realities of the gospel, written and directed by Jesus himself. The bread and wine in the Lord's Supper portray Christ's body and blood broken and poured out for the remission of our sins, a visual reminder of Christ's cross work on our behalf (Luke 22:19–20). In the same way, baptism portrays our spiritual death to sin, our symbolic burial with Christ, and our resurrection with him to new life (Rom. 6:3–4). The ordinances, then, are where we see the gospel enacted and our participation in it dramatized. They are where the Word of God's promise is spoken to us in tangible form—we touch and taste the bread and wine; we feel the waters of baptism. They are means of grace instituted by Jesus that God uses to assure his people of the trustworthiness of his gospel and the reality of our participation in it.[10]

The ordinances are the visible signs and seals of participation in the new covenant. After the right preaching of the Word, the right administration of the sacraments is what most visibly marks out the church from the world. So it is especially important that the pastor is faithful here. In part, faithfulness in administering the ordinances means requiring baptism for church membership. Baptism is the physical representation of spiritual conversion. It is the first external sign of membership in the new covenant, identifying us with the people of God. As such, it should be the first external requirement for membership in the church.

Faithfulness here also implies that we are exercising church discipline when necessary—ultimately protecting people from taking the Lord's Supper if they are currently involved in scandalous, unrepented sin, or if they are reasonably suspected of hiding unrepented sin by prolonged neglect of church attendance. Such sins call into question the genuineness of a member's profession. The conscientious pastor will, by protectively barring that member from the table, warn such a person that a person "eats and drinks judgment to himself if he does not judge the body rightly" (1 Cor. 11:29).

Taking such care in our administration of the ordinances will help prevent false conversions, protect the regenerate nature of our church's membership, preclude unrestrained immorality, and thus preempt charges of hypocrisy, making our evangelism more winsome and more consistent with our witness.

Think Tank

1. Do your Sunday morning church services include all five elements of worship (read, preach, pray, sing, and see the Word)? If not, why not?

2. How can you start working to incorporate the elements that aren't currently present?

3. Are the ordinances playing their proper role in your church? Has anything else replaced them?

On Multiple Services

Another way we "see the Bible" is in the corporate life of the congregation lived out together. Many today believe that a church can do all the above things even more effectively using multiple Sunday morning services. Some employ multiple services to offer multiple styles of worship music as a means of attracting more people. Others have already experienced such explosive numerical growth that a multiple-service format seems to be the only answer that practically accommodates the windfall. The church I serve in Washington, DC, Capitol Hill Baptist, is facing some of these same growing pains as I write.

Recognizing wide room for disagreement, enjoying close fellowship with churches that have multiple Sunday services, and experiencing the logistical difficulties that sometimes make multiple services seem inevitable, we are still reluctant to use a multiple-service format for the Sunday morning gathering.

The main reason is that the church is just that—a gathering. The Greek word for "church" is *ekklēsia*, which in the New Testament also refers to a single gathering of people who are not the people of God.[11] By definition and by use, an *ekklēsia* is a corporate singularity—one group of people who are all in the same place at the same time. The very definition of the word "church," then, makes it difficult to embrace multiple services as a format for the main weekly "gathering" of church members. Are multiple gatherings the best way to reflect the corporate unity or singularity of the church? Are they the best way to facilitate the singular gathering of the people of God in the same place at the same time? Might multiple gatherings actually constitute multiple churches?

The way both Luke and Paul talk about the corporate gatherings of the church, it sounds as if everyone in the church is present. Even with a church of three thousand members, "all [*pantes*] the believers were together" and "every day they [all the believers] continued to meet together [*homothumadon*] in the temple courts" (Acts 2:44, 46 NIV 1984).[12] Luke remembered that "all the believers used to meet together [*homothumadon hapantes*] in Solomon's Colonnade" (5:12 NIV 1984). In Acts 15:22 (NIV 1984) "the apostles and elders, with the whole church" [*sun holē tē ekklēsia*] decided to send Paul and Barnabas to Antioch. And in 1 Corinthians 14, where Paul intends to provide authoritative teaching on order in the corporate assembly, he sets the scene by saying, "Therefore if the whole church assembles together [*ean oun sunelthē hē ekklēsia holē*] . . . " (v. 23).[13]

It is interesting, too, that many of the biblical images for the church are corporate unities. The local church is variously referred to as one flock comprised of many sheep (Acts 20:28), one body comprised of many members (1 Cor. 12:14–27), one temple comprised of many stones (Eph. 2:19–22), and one household comprised of many members (Eph. 2:19).

Again, recognizing and even experiencing all the difficulties that come with numerical growth in a landlocked downtown location, limiting ourselves to a one-service format for the main weekly gathering on Sunday morning seems like a good and necessary implication of the biblical data.

All this having been said, if the church you serve holds multiple services, it would be wise to make haste *slowly* in moving toward one service. Teach. Cultivate broad-based unity of mind, first among other leaders, and then, through them, among the congregation at large. This is not an issue over which you should split the church! This is a persuasion-level belief. It is not a conviction, like the divinity of Christ, over which we should break fellowship upon disagreement. Nor is it a mere opinion, like what color the carpet should be. It is a persuasion—we've evaluated the biblical data and have been persuaded that a particular conclusion is warranted. Even though it is not a matter that touches the doctrine of salvation, it is still a matter of some importance addressed sparsely—yet we believe consistently—in Scripture. We may seek to persuade others, as we have done here, for the edification of the church. But to fracture church unity over a matter like this would be unwarranted.

8

The Role of the Pastor

NOW THAT WE'VE INTRODUCED both a specific understanding of the church[1] and a specific model of corporate worship (see chaps. 6–7), it is time to think more particularly about the pastor's role, both in the leadership of the church generally and in the corporate worship gathering of the local church.

Practitioner of the Marks

As we discovered in the Introduction, the uniqueness of the church is in its gospel message, which is dramatized in the ordinances of baptism and the Lord's Supper. Not surprisingly, the sixteenth-century Reformers were eager, on those grounds, to define the true church in terms of the right preaching of the Word and the right administration of the ordinances.

The nature of the true church, in turn, has important implications for the nature of a true pastor. If the true church distinguishes itself from the world and from false churches by preaching and the ordinances, then it makes sense that the most visible leader of the church should be a practitioner of those marks. In other words, the pastor should be leading in a way that leads the church to be the church.[2]

The most important and fundamental role of the pastor is to preach the gospel clearly. The primacy of preaching will never change, no matter what stage of life the church is in. Whether your church is six months old or sixty years old, whether the pastor has five years or fifty years of experience, whether the church has five or five thousand members, preaching will always be primary because the church is distinguished from the world by living on every word that comes from the mouth of God (Matt. 4:4). While we never want to drive a wedge between preaching and the ordinances, it is still appropriate to say that the preaching of the gospel even takes primacy over the ordinances because it is the preaching of the gospel that informs our understanding of what is symbolized in baptism and the Lord's Supper.

This, however, in no way denigrates the importance of rightly administering the ordinances. Rightly administering baptism and the Lord's Supper is crucial to pastoral faithfulness. This is because, broadly speaking, baptism tends the front door of the church, while the Lord's Supper tends the back door. Properly administered baptism (i.e., baptism of believers only upon a credible profession of faith) helps to ensure that only genuine believers are admitted into the membership of the church. Properly administered communion (i.e., communion given only to members in good standing of evangelical churches) helps to ensure that those who are under church discipline for unrepented sin do not scandalize the church or eat and drink judgment to themselves by partaking of the Lord's Supper (1 Cor. 11:29).

Teaching Is Everything

Teaching is everything. I do not mean that teaching is the only thing that a pastor should do. Nor do I advocate some lifeless orthodoxy. What I mean is that everything that happens up front in a corporate worship gathering is part of the teaching ministry of the church. Everything teaches, whether you intend it to or not. The songs teach people doctrine and proper affections for God. Your prayers (or lack of them) teach people how to pray themselves. The kinds of prayers you pray (or don't pray) teach people about the important differences between prayers of adoration, confession, thanksgiving, and supplication. The way you administer the ordinances teaches people about their meaning, and even the very meaning of the gospel. Your preaching teaches people how to study and use the Bible appropriately. Everything from the call to worship to the benediction counts as teaching. Teaching is everything.

If you are the main preaching pastor at your church, then God will in some way hold you accountable for everything that happens up front in the corporate worship gatherings of your church. Part of your role, then, is to be as intentional and deliberate as you can about planning those services in a way that conforms to the God centeredness and gospel centeredness of the church. Be hands-on in planning corporate worship services. Choose hymns and worship choruses that are rich with the glories of God's character and works, that raise our gaze from ourselves and our own concerns to Christ and his cross. Choose music that serves the intention of God-centered lyrics and draws attention to the work of the Spirit in the life of the church.[3]

In leading the Sunday morning service, pray prayers that are saturated with rightly used Scripture—perhaps even one of the Scripture passages to be read aloud in the service or the passage to be preached on that morning. Include prayers of corporate adoration, confession, thanksgiving, and supplication so that you can model a healthy individual prayer life for the congregation. Preach sermons that submit themselves to the main point that the passage is making so that they model responsible Bible study and application. Let the main theological theme of the passage being preached be present in the songs that are sung and even in some of the prayers that are prayed.

What this will mean for your ministry is that you will periodically need to devote time on your calendar (two or three days) to planning services ahead of time—maybe three or four months of services at a time. This will be hard work at first, but it will free you up to create whole services that display thematic continuity, and will also free you up from the pressure of planning services week by week as they come.

Think Tank

1. What are the pastor's two primary responsibilities? Why is this so, biblically?

2. What other demands encroach on a pastor's primary responsibilities? Why does this happen?

3. What are some ways you can keep those other demands from crowding out the main ones?

4. Why do you plan your corporate worship services the way you do? Is there need for change?

The Day-to-Day

"So what do you do all week?" Ah, if only they knew. If you are a senior pastor, then much of your time should be invested in preparing the public teaching of the church. "Preach the word" is your fundamental biblical mandate (2 Tim. 4:2). It is not at all odd, especially for young or new pastors, to spend twenty-five hours per week in sermon preparation and study for other teaching opportunities. Exposition is difficult, glorious work. The senior pastor also prepares for and leads staff meetings, attends elders' meetings, and visits and disciples the congregation—not to mention the myriad conversations (pleasant and otherwise) a pastor is called to navigate during the week. Since most of these responsibilities are handled elsewhere, let's concentrate here on running a godly and helpful staff meeting.

As the church grows, and your need for supporting staff increases, the senior pastor will need to be the one who keeps everyone on the same page and oversees the ministries of the other staff members. In leading staff meetings, it's helpful to begin by reading and praying through *Scripture*—usually the passage to be preached the following

Sunday. It is also wise to include a brief time of *prayer for the congregation*—perhaps just one page of the membership directory each week, trusting that the whole staff is committed to praying through a page every day in their own personal time with the Lord. You might think of brief encouraging articles to hand out and have people read as a regular part of *staff development and team building.* You may even take time occasionally to ask opinions on a current issue or article that touches the church, giving the staff an opportunity to think through a practical or theological issue together for a few minutes. Or you might periodically bless the staff with a particularly encouraging biography or theological book for their own spiritual encouragement and enjoyment.

It will be helpful for you, as well, to have some system that keeps you abreast of what people are doing without making them feel badgered. Weekly *staff reports* can be a great tool—I receive them from our staff members each week. But if you decide to expect them from the staff, make sure to avoid making people feel that you have unrealistic expectations. Provide direction and set a hard-working pace, but communicate generous amounts of grace and patience as you go. Create a gracious and appreciative atmosphere among the staff. Lead in expressing gratitude. Model trust in God's sovereignty by being slow to frustration and impatience in conversations with members. None of these spiritual characteristics come naturally to sinful people like us. Pray that the Lord would enable you by his Spirit to grow and lead in this way.

The staff meeting is also the best time to nail down *calendar items.* These will include items that have to do with the corporate life of the church, like upcoming members' meetings, new members' classes, baptisms, communion services, conferences, or the like. They will also include staff coordination items, like who's preaching or teaching in different services, who is teaching a new members' class, who is responsible for conducting an upcoming wedding or funeral, who will follow up on certain decisions and details regarding conversations with particular members, who will research or write a certain adult education curriculum, who is going on vacation when, which ministries need replacement leaders, when will the pastor have outside speaking engagements, and a host of other items.

This is a lot to cover. At the same time, it's good to keep staff meetings as brief and encouraging as possible. So try to keep things moving at a brisk but happy pace. Resentment can sometimes quietly build if staff meetings drone on and on, no matter how encouraging you think they may be. Two hours should be the absolute max, especially if you're meeting every week.

Regarding the pastor's weekly schedule in general, I'd encourage you to observe discipline. "Discipline yourself for the purpose of godliness" (1 Tim. 4:7). Set a schedule and keep to it. Get into a healthy routine. Set weekly and even monthly or quarterly times of sermon preparation, study for other biblical teaching, prayer for yourself and the congregation, organization, conversation (discipling, counseling, returning phone calls), visiting (hospitals, in-home visits, etc.), developmental reading, service planning, and whatever other pastoral duties to which the Lord might call you. He who fails to plan, plans to fail. Take time now to decide when you will do these things during the week, month, or year. Put it on the calendar and follow through as the Lord enables you. Otherwise, ministry can sprawl out formlessly all over the place and present challenges to our families and ministries that could be tamed with better forethought and self-discipline.

God has entrusted you with only a finite number of hours and days. Steward them well to his glory, the health of your family, and the edification of the church.

The Three G's

Pastoral ministry can be summed up with three general obligations: graze, guide, and guard.

Graze. The pastor's first responsibility is to feed the sheep on the Word of God (John 21:15–17; 2 Tim. 4:2). A shepherd simply cannot be faithful to his task if he doesn't feed his flock well (Ezek. 34:2–3, 13–14; 1 Tim. 3:2; Titus 1:9). He must provide them with green pastures in which to lie down and graze (Ps. 23:1–2). Make sure there is both milk for the newborn (1 Pet. 2:2) and meat for the mature (Heb. 5:11–14). Clarify the gospel for unbelievers and nominal Christians, and clarify its continuing implications for genuine believers.[4] A man may have a charismatic personality; he may be a gifted administrator and a skillful orator; he may be armed with an impressive program; he may even have the people skills of a politician and the empathic listening skills of a counselor; but he will starve the sheep if he cannot feed the people of God on the Word of God. Programs and personalities are dispensable. But without food, sheep die.[5] Feeding the flock is therefore the pastor's first priority. "Feed my lambs" (John 21:15 ESV).

Guide. Sheep need to be led, not just fed (Ps. 23:3–4). Leading sheep means we must be out in front so that they can follow us to the green pastures. This, in turn, means that we must be initiating godly conversations and strategizing for the spread of the gospel, as well as setting godly examples in the way we live and lead (1 Tim. 4:12; 1 Pet. 5:1–5). Leadership in the church also means equipping people with what they need for spiritual growth and ministry (Eph. 4:11–13), and serving them in a way that cultivates a culture of servant leadership and emulates the ethos of the Savior (Mark 10:45; John 13:1–17). Not least of the guiding functions is to keep the sheep together and to bring back the strays (Ezek. 34:4–12, 16). This guiding function, however, can be performed in a godly way only as the pastor himself is watching his own life and doctrine closely (1 Tim. 4:16). All will be lost if the pastor's self-watch is neglected.

Guard. A faithful shepherd is always on the watch against predators and will put himself in harm's way on behalf of the flock when the need arises (John 10:12–15). Most of these predators will come in the form of teachers who twist the truth (Acts 20:28–31), which is why pastors and elders are called to be men who can "encourage others in sound doctrine and refute those who oppose it" (Titus 1:9 NIV 1984). Sometimes we must be the ones who know how to defuse a potentially divisive situation. Other times we are called to engage in doctrinal battle over significant issues—those that affect the gospel and the security of the church in it. When that happens, it is part of our protective responsibility to the local church we serve to engage in doctrinal controversy for the clarity of the gospel and the health of the church. In this way, we not only guard the flock, but we guard the "treasure which has been entrusted" to us (2 Tim. 1:14).

9

Evangelistic Exposition

WE TEND TO THINK OF expositional preaching and evangelistic preaching as opposites, or at least incompatible. But shouldn't all Christian preaching both expound God's Word and proclaim his gospel? Jesus thought so. As early as Mark 2, he preaches himself as the Bridegroom, the Son of Man, and the Lord of the Sabbath. In other words, he exposes those Old Testament texts and themes as fulfilled in his own person and work—he exposits them evangelistically. In fact, this was Jesus's understanding of the whole Old Testament. "Then He opened their minds so they could understand the Scriptures. He told them, 'This is what is written: That Christ will suffer and rise from the dead on the third day, and repentance and forgiveness of sins will be preached in his name to all nations, beginning at Jerusalem" (Luke 24:45–47 NIV 1984). That's not a quote from any specific text; it's Jesus's own summary of Genesis to Malachi.

Time and again in the book of Acts, the apostles' sermons followed that same pattern. Acts 2 expounds Joel 2 as fulfilled in gospel events. Acts 3 proclaims Jesus as the promised prophet of Deuteronomy 18. Acts 13 expounds the gospel implications of Psalms 2 and 16, and Isaiah 49. "What God promised to the fathers, this he has fulfilled to us their children by raising Jesus, as also it is written in the second

Psalm . . . " (Acts 13:32–33). From synagogue to marketplace, Paul regularly reasons from the Scriptures that Jesus is the promised Christ—expository evangelism, evangelistic exposition. Peter summarizes the message of the prophets as "the sufferings of Christ and the glories to follow" (1 Pet. 1:10–12). And Paul expounds Genesis 15:6, in both Galatians 3 and Romans 4, as fulfilled in Christ. The dominical and apostolic pattern is to declare all of God's Word to all of God's people, pointing us all to the fulfillment of God's promises in Christ (2 Cor. 1:20).

What Expositional Preaching Does

Expositional preaching takes the point of the passage and makes *that* the point of the sermon. It exposes what's there in God's Word—patiently, methodically, honestly—and applies it to those who hear. Of course, Christians need to be fed on such a regular diet of biblical exposition (Deut. 8:3). But non-Christians need to be addressed by the point of God's Word as well—patiently, methodically, honestly. One of the great benefits of expositional preaching through books of the Bible is that it gives non-Christians extended time to learn what the Bible says in context.

In an age of biblical illiteracy and worldview confusion, clear evangelism often needs to be every bit as patient and painstaking as the upbuilding of existing believers. Unbelievers have normally been steeped in a lifetime of their own sin and Satan's lies. Meanwhile, God is famous for working slowly. It should be no surprise, then, that he often takes weeks and months (sometimes years!) to convince non-Christians of his truth, convict them of sin, teach them of his authority over creation, unveil his design for marriage and sex, for work and worship—and to bring them to lasting repentance from sin and faith in Jesus.

Expositional preaching is perfectly poised to confront unbelievers with God's logic and law, God's will and wrath, and God's grace to cover their guilt. By exposing the text of Scripture, biblical exposition unsheathes the only blade sharp enough to pierce the thoughts and intentions of a self-deceived heart (Heb. 4:12).

Of course, biblical exposition without the biblical gospel won't save or edify anyone. Faith comes from hearing, and hearing from *the Word of Christ* (Rom. 10:17). Christless preaching fails to present anyone with the only person powerful enough to save. Our preaching, then, must present the gospel! But what counts as an evangelistic sermon?

What Evangelistic Sermons Are

Some say evangelistic sermons have to be dramatic and emotional. Others are convinced they have to be seeker sensitive—dense with idiom, aimed at felt needs, lightened with humor and human interest. Still others confuse evangelistic preaching with explanatory apologetics, or see it as inseparable from planned revival services. To some, whatever preaching meets with evident success in conversions is evangelistic—and whatever doesn't, isn't. But neither style, setting, nor success determines whether a sermon is evangelistic. That honor belongs to the evangel alone.

It is the content of the sermon that determines its character. Is the gospel clear and central? Then, and then alone, is the sermon truly evangelistic. Better, is the gospel presented as arising demonstrably from the words, themes, characters, and images of the text being preached? Then it's evangelistic *exposition*. Better still, is the gospel pressed home to the heart with urgency, charity, clarity, and sincerity, for the salvation of sinners and the strengthening of saints? Then it's evangelistic expositional *preaching*.

But if we preach evangelistically in our churches, aren't we just preaching to the choir? Maybe, but even singers sin. The Puritan preacher William Perkins observed long ago that churches have "both believers and unbelievers. This is the typical situation in our congregations."[1] One category we need to recover is "the unregenerate church member." Careful as our membership practices may be, we have to admit that only Jesus can read people's hearts (Jer. 17:9–10). Some of our members can live for years in the soundest of churches unconcerned about their sins and unconverted in their souls. This reality would be reason enough for evangelistic exposition.

But sound evangelistic preaching is helpful for genuine Christians, too. Think of how Paul taught the Galatians to continue in the gospel as they had begun (Gal. 3:1–6). And besides, where is the Christian among us who has no room to grow in comprehending God's love, obeying his commands, trusting Christ's blood and righteousness, persevering in hardship, and hoping for heaven? The gospel of Christ's suffering and glory encourages us along the way to the Celestial City as we carry our own crosses in discipleship to Christ. Evangelistic exposition, then, doesn't just inform and confront the unbeliever; it fortifies the faithful. It puts our suffering in the context of Christ's. It makes Christ's suffering more dear to our hearts. It warns us of the dangers along the way. It exalts Jesus as our all-sufficient Savior and Lord. And in all these ways it elicits our praise to Christ as we grow in our understanding and appreciation for who Jesus is and all he has accomplished for us in his life, death, resurrection, and ascension.

Evangelistic exposition is also good for Christians because it helps them integrate biblical truth into their everyday lives. The gospel becomes the standard for truth, the filter for behavior, and a fence against sin. As we grow in the knowledge of God's holiness, we respect and fear his fatherly displeasure—we sin less because we love more. His greatness becomes the ground of our faith, and his truth the anchor of our trust in his Word. His creation of the world, and of us in his image, teaches us to carry out our vocations in ways that please and honor him.

As a result, evangelistic exposition encourages an organic kind of faithfulness in personal evangelism. As the evangel becomes more central in our sermons, evangelism becomes more natural for those who hear us—and for us ourselves as preachers! When we preach the gospel organically from all of Scripture, and apply it to all of life, Christians slowly learn to apply the gospel organically to this popular movie or that pointed editorial; to this thorny ethical dilemma or that snarky tweet. Printed evangelistic tracts can be great tools. But when we're with our unbelieving friends and family members, organic transitions to the gospel are priceless. Evangelistic exposition trains Christians over time to see the gospel connections that address our world and lead to evangelistic conversations that are more faithful than forced.

How to Preach Expositional Sermons Evangelistically

How then do we preach expositional sermons evangelistically? One place to look for an answer is the preaching of men like James Montgomery Boice through Genesis or D. Martyn Lloyd-Jones in Ephesians. Sometimes it's caught before it's taught.

But we also need to see that the whole Bible is gospel shaped. We see everywhere the Christ-centered themes of creation, decreation, and new creation; exodus and new exodus; sin, sacrifice, and substitution; prophet, priest, and king; salvation through judgment; life through death and resurrection; exile and return; and many others. God is consistently revealing, all throughout the Bible, his own character and expectations, why he created us, how we've rebelled against his law and rejected his love, what he's done for us to reconcile us to himself in Christ, the categories Jesus would fulfill for us, and God's call for us to repent of our sins and trust in Jesus for forgiveness and newness of life in the power of his Spirit. Understanding our Bibles in this way protects us from mere moralizing and enables us to preach not simply what people ought to do, but what Christ did that we could never do.

With these things in mind, there are a few ways we can make our expositions evangelistic.

1. *Preach with Non-Believers in Mind:* First, we can be *accommodating* to non-Christian visitors. To be sure, the purpose of the main weekly gathering is edification of the saints, not evangelism (1 Cor. 14). Jesus charges us to feed his sheep. As we do that, by God's grace, Christians

become more evangelistic and they bring their non-Christian friends to church to hear the gospel.

Therefore, we're wise to periodically explain why we do what we do in our services, so that both believers and unbelievers can follow the service well. We can also use nontechnical language unbelievers can understand. We can orient people to the Bible, perhaps explaining how chapter and verse numbers work or directing them to a page number in the pew Bible. And we can use a modern translation that's readable.

2. *Use Sermon Titles:* We can also use our sermon *titles* to incite interest and invite attention. Coaxing interest need not compromise content. Think about why God has spoken your preaching text to our hearts. What condition is he addressing? What error is he correcting? What truth is he teaching? Why do we need to hear what he says? What promise or hope is he holding out to us? Series and sermon titles can provide a teaser to the content of the text and hint at how it will intersect with people's thoughts, feelings, assumptions, worldviews, and relationships. Series and sermon titles can function like truthful advertisements.

3. *Use Sermon Introductions:* Sermon *introductions* can also be useful tools to demonstrate why people, Christian or not, should listen to the sermon. It's convenient to assume everyone's as interested in our sermons as we are, but of course we know that people come to church distracted or despairing, sad or mad, tired, apathetic, even cynical at times. Whether it's a compelling question, a provocative statement, a pointed illustration, or an illustrative quote from a recent editorial, thoughtfulness in how you begin can often serve to arrest and hold attention all the way through to the end.

4. *Preach Doctrinally:* But first you'll need to give your own attention to the concepts you're introducing. What biblical *doctrine* does your passage teach? What worldview does it address? And how does your text itself preach the simple gospel truths of God's holiness, our sin and its consequences, Christ's death and resurrection, and the call to

repent and believe? Presenting a clear, concise summary of the gospel as it arises from your preaching text in each of your expositions can help ensure that you're preaching evangelistically. Consider something like this:

> This holy Creator made us to love and serve him forever. Sadly, we rebelled against his law and rejected his love—we sinned against him. We might ignore him for now, but we cannot avoid him forever. One day, God's patience with sinners will end, and his judgment will begin. Then we will give an account to him, and he will rightly judge us for our sins. Our only defense will be in Christ's righteousness and sacrifice. God himself sent his eternal Son to become a man, in order to live the sinless life we should have lived, and then to die the death we deserved, in our place, for our sins, on the cross. There he bore God's condemnation for all the sins of all his people. Jesus suffered our sentence at God's own command. But God raised him from the dead to prove Jesus died not for any sin of his own, but for ours. And God accepted Jesus back to heaven's throne to demonstrate his acceptance of Jesus's sacrifice for our forgiveness. God's righteous anger toward those in Christ has been exhausted on Christ. Based on this provision of mercy and promise of hope, God commands us all to confess our sins to him, repent of our rebellion, and trust in Christ to find reconciliation with God and new life in Jesus.

You might shorten some aspects of this explanation and elaborate on others, based on which of these themes is most prominent in your preaching text. Whatever the case, some gospel summary like this should be clear in every exposition. But this summary should not be offered as an option to be considered or a solution to a felt need. After all, we don't always feel our greatest needs or choose the best options. Rather, we announce this gospel as the summons of the almighty Judge. We know with certainty that none of our hearers will be able to justify themselves before God based on their works. As such, our unbelieving listeners are in danger of an eternal hell if they refuse to repent. We, then, are accountable to God for notifying others, by our preaching, that they are accountable to God. It is far better, then, for all concerned that we be clear rather than coy (see Mark 8:38; Acts 17:31; Rom. 3:19–20; Heb. 9:27).

5. *Use Illustrations:* When Paul quoted Greek inscriptions and poets to the Athenians in Acts 17, he demonstrated the value of *illustration*. Of course, no illustration can substitute for a clear presentation of the gospel. But popular books, films, editorials, and political situations can help our non-Christian friends see how countless gospel themes intersect with their lives, confront their sins, and contradict their own worldviews. A pointed personal testimony, whether contemporary or historical, can also help press gospel truth home to the heart. Illustration should not dwarf exposition, and illustrations from your own life should not be self-exalting, but God is honored when his gospel is demonstrated as true; so illustrate the gospel's power in your preaching.

6. *Apply the Text:* But our *applications* should be just as evangelistic as our illustrations. This means we'll have to be clear and courageous with our hearers about sin. A good doctor has to be right and honest about the diagnosis before he can issue the right prescription. Just so, the Great Physician has diagnosed humanity with sin, and it is a pandemic. Yet the contagion can incubate undetected. In fact, most of our patients consider themselves asymptomatic.

God has designed evangelistic exposition to function as a diagnostic that can reveal for sinners the heart disease they don't even realize has infected them (Heb. 4:12). We become deceptive doctors of the soul when we grow more concerned with how our bedside manner is received than with the correct diagnosis and prescription. We are not trying to win the non-Christian's approval. We are trying to win their souls. Setting a broken bone is painful. No patient wants to need that treatment. But for a doctor to deny the need for such treatment in necessary cases is neither wisdom nor compassion; it's malfeasance.

For personal accountability, then, we can think of five kinds of expositional applications.[2] You might make a grid with rows across for each point of the sermon (on the left) and columns down for kinds of application in each point (at the top). The columns can help you consider first what's unique to salvation history, then how the text applies uniquely to Christ as fulfilled in his person and work. Next we can think about how the text calls the non-Christian to repent of sinful actions or attitudes, or to trust in Christ and the gospel. We should also consider how the text applies to the life of the individual Christian in the public square, living in the world but not of it. Finally, we can meditate on how the text applies to our individual Christian lives, and also to the corporate life and health of our shared life together in the local church.

We won't always follow the same order in our study, or even get to all of these different kinds of application in each point of every sermon. But it's a good discipline to ensure that we're thinking not only in terms of edifying believers, but also in terms of evangelizing unbelievers in our regular preaching of God's Word. As we think of these evangelistic applications, we might do well to ask how this verse or that point will sound to a non-Christian friend, and then to craft an application that directly addresses the unbeliever's sin, misconception, evasion, or despair.

Here again, though, it's important to remember that we're not simply tacking on the same boilerplate gospel presentation to every sermon. Ideally, we're presenting the gospel from the organic emphases of the passage we're preaching. For example, if we're preaching Joshua 2 or 6, we don't preach Christ's blood from the redness of Rahab's scarlet cord. But she does hear the gospel of God's freeing his people from Egypt, she fears God's judgment, she repents of her former worldview and her false worship, and she casts in her lot with the people of God. As a result, she experiences the same kind of protection from God's judgment as the

Israelites did at the very first Passover in Exodus 12, and for the same reasons—she hears and believes God's warning of judgment and his promise of salvation. That's the gospel according to Rahab.

But our hearers have to know how to respond to the gospel we preach, and that's why an *invitation* is crucial. As an organic part of the sermon itself, the preacher calls sinners to confess their sins, repent of them, submit to the kingship of Christ Jesus, and trust in his death and resurrection for forgiveness and salvation. "Sinner, repent and believe." That kind of call should be common in our preaching. In addition, we can invite non-Christians to talk with us after the service or encourage them to speak with the Christian friend who brought them. It's best to avoid any kind of invitation that would lead them to think that in responding to our invitation they've responded savingly to Christ. That is a well-intentioned mistake that leads to confusion and carnality in the churches. Yet with every caution noted, we must still call people to respond to the gospel, not just to hear it.

Think Tank

1. What are some elements that can help us preach expositional sermons evangelistically?

2. How might your next expositional sermon exalt Christ better by exploring the text's connection to gospel themes?

3. How might your next evangelistic sermon be strengthened and clarified by proclaiming one text expositionally?

10

The Roles of the Different Gatherings

NUTRITIONISTS COMMONLY RECOGNIZE that the five different food groups each sustain the body in a unique but harmonious way. If we want to be healthy, we need to be eating a combination of foods that span the five groups. We can't just eat bread and ice cream and expect to stay fit and trim! It's similar with the different gatherings of the church; each one will ideally perform a different role in the cultivation of corporate health—holiness, love, and sound doctrine.

What follows in this chapter is not intended as the "be all and end all" of weekly service planning. It is merely offered as an example of how you could use the different weekly gatherings effectively to cultivate health in a local church. This is the model we've used at our church in Washington, DC, and we've done so with great benefit, by God's grace.

Adult Education Hour

The adult education hour is the main *equipping* time. Many see this as a time for age-graded fellowship or teaching that is related to a particular stage of life. As popular as this model is, we think the adult education hour can offer something much more unique and helpful than age-graded fellowship.

Affinity-based fellowship is often duplicated in weekly Bible studies. What's missing from many local churches, however, is an integrated system of teaching that begins to equip members in the areas of basic Christianity for starters, living the Christian life, Old and New Testament overviews, systematic theology, church history, and Christian growth. The idea is to provide people with a growing backpack of resources for understanding the Bible more accurately and living the Christian life more faithfully. When a person has completed all the classes (which may take up to four or five years, depending on the amount of material offered), then he is encouraged to attend the adult education classes with a younger Christian friend, or even a teenaged son or daughter. The class can then be used as a tool that might spur fruitful discipling conversations during the week. You could think of the class selection along the lines of a college curriculum and make related reading materials available for those who would like to supplement their learning or who might be interested in teaching the class in the future. For older members, attending the classes multiple times over the years might seem redundant. But constant improvements to the teaching materials, additions to the curriculum, a variety of supplemental reading, and the change of role from student to active discipler would break any perceived monotony.

Sunday Morning Service

The Sunday morning service is the main *feeding* time. As such, biblical exposition is primary. It is popular to view this service primarily as an evangelistic time. As a result, many churches are calibrating these services to the musical and cultural preferences of their target audiences. According to 1 Corinthians 14, though, the purpose of the main weekly gathering of the church is not evangelism but edification.[1] It seems wise, then, to calibrate these services not to the preferences of unbelievers, but to the scriptural parameters given to us for the mutual edification of believers.

This is also the main weekly worship gathering of the church. Since worship is a response to revelation, this is where the meatiest expositional meal is served. As the main corporate feeding time for the gathered congregation, biblical exposition is the centerpiece not only of this service, but of the entire public ministry of the Word. Yet since all Scripture is about Christ (Luke 24:25–27, 45–47), that exposition should always lead to an unearthing of the evangel. This means that the sermon should normally be an *evangelistic exposition*—it should expose both believers and unbelievers to the content of the gospel and its implications for each as the natural result of making the point of the passage the point of the message. Such preaching will help motivate members to bring their unbelieving friends because they know the gospel will be clearly presented and unbelievers will be openly exhorted to repent and believe. This evangelistic exposition will be best complemented by thoughtfully chosen Scripture readings, carefully worded prayers, and meaningful songs that all underline the theme of the passage.

In short, this is where we read, preach, pray, sing, and see the Word of God together every week.[2] But again, that doesn't just happen spontaneously. We have to plan for it. It's worth giving significant chunks of time to thinking through which songs to sing and Scripture passages to read, based on which sermon text you'll be preaching. This kind of thoughtfulness can give the whole service a sense of cohesion, which can make the public gathering easier to follow—especially when it's led well from up front.

When I'm attending my home church but not preaching, I love to be the one to lead the Sunday morning service. It gives me an opportunity to relate to the whole gathered congregation not primarily as preacher, but more specifically as a teaching shepherd who leads them by the hand through the public service so that they can follow along and feed freely without worrying about getting lost—kind of like leading them into the green pastures. I also love to train and equip other elders and leaders to lead our public services so that more men in the church can develop a voice of loving authority that can serve as a steady guide for the congregation during our gathered worship.

Service leading is a great opportunity to explain what we're doing in the service, why we're doing a particular thing, and why we're doing it in that way. At its best, service leading teaches the "whys" behind our "hows," and helps the congregation follow our lead in the public ministry of the Word.

Leading a service with forethought, wisdom, and love can teach the congregation, and our unbelieving visitors, how to make sense of the whole service as we move through it together. At a nuts-and-bolts level, it involves introducing the songs we'll sing and the readings we'll hear so that together we understand how every element either prepares us to hear the sermon text or facilitates our response to it. Just a few brief sentences to explain the song we're about to sing or the reading we're about to hear and how it relates to the sermon (or to other elements in the service) can help the congregation engage it with their whole mind.

Another great utility of thoughtful service leading is that it prevents the congregation from developing a wrong kind of traditionalism that says, "We've just always done it this way, but we don't know why." It's healthy when our congregations know why we do things the way we do them. Thoughtful service leading can even provide a winsome rationale for our order of worship to our unbelieving visitors, and help them navigate their way through unfamiliar waters.

Sunday Evening Service

The Sunday evening service is the main *family* time of the church. It would be easy to plan the Sunday evening service as a sort of "Sunday Morning Lite"—same elements, same ratios of music to prayer and prayer to preaching—but in a compressed time frame and more casual atmosphere. But this service may be better used to develop the mutual concern and familial closeness that nurtures selfless Christian community.

Sunday evening gatherings have fallen on hard times lately. After all, Scripture never specifically commands us to gather more than once on the Lord's Day. But it's worth remembering that Jesus taught us to pray the Lord's Prayer in the first person plural—our, us, we, not I, my, me. It would seem that Jesus wants us to at least remember that we are individually a part of a corporate body. Maybe that's why the early church modeled gathered corporate prayer so faithfully (Acts 1:14; 2:42; 4:24, 31; 6:12; 12:5). Paul even commands the churches to pray together as churches (Rom. 12:12; 15:30; 1 Cor. 11; Col. 4:2; 1 Tim. 2:8).

So how do you go about leading a service designed to facilitate corporate prayer, family closeness, and an emphasis on gospel-oriented concerns in our shared prayer life? Here's what we do (it's not perfect, but it's a start). We begin with God-centered songs of fellowship, which are followed by a brief prayer and then a short time of announcements concerning body life. We then try to move seamlessly into a time of taking briefly stated prayer requests from members of the congregation. These are usually cleared with the pastor beforehand to ensure that the requests are appropriate. In other words, we want to be intentional about gradually moving the congregation away from just praying for the physical needs of members and nonmembers, and toward praying for the spiritual needs of members, their own spiritual needs, evangelistic opportunities, and prospects for local church planting and international missions. We're encouraging members to be open about both their spiritual needs and their ministry opportunities, and to embrace a prayerful concern for the needs and opportunities of others in the congregation. For each request shared, a brief prayer is prayed by a member who volunteers (or is asked to do so). Then a brief (ten- to fifteen-minute) devotional sermon is given by either an elder or a young man preparing for pastoral ministry. The passage preached is on the same theme as the morning sermon, but from the other Testament. We sing a final song or hymn and end with a brief time of silence for reflection on the point of the devotional. Total length is usually an hour and a half. And we make it clear to people when they are joining the church that we expect them normally to attend this meeting.

Another fruitful way to use a Sunday evening service is to incorporate a time of congregational conversation and prayer over applications from the sermon text that was preached in the morning service. Over time, this habit can give the saints practice at talking and praying together about Scripture and its implications for us. It can also serve as a pastoral instrument for measuring how well people are understanding and applying our sermons. Assuming you have a good relationship with the congregation, you might even periodically open the floor for questions about the morning sermon text. That can give you an opportunity to model humility, patience, approachability, and remedial care.

This service is one of the biggest corporate ways that we aim to be intentional about loving each other and engaging in each other's lives. In this way, we are aiming to use the Sunday evening service to cultivate the corporate health and witness of the local church. When I started the Sunday evening service, it was very sparsely attended for the first year or two. But it has steadily grown and now is one of the most significant parts of our weekly life together as a church. Persistence pays off! Over the last twenty years, we've seen this become a particularly warm and sweet time, as evangelistic opportunities are shared, marital engagements are announced, fruit from ministry opportunities is prayed for, members out of the area are lifted up, missionaries are remembered and prayed for, births are announced, and young pastors are sent out. In fact, we often hear the comment from newer members that they started coming for the preaching, but they decided to become members because of experiencing the family life and love on Sunday nights.

If you try to start a Sunday evening gathering where none previously existed, or you're re-starting it after a long period of neglect, be determined. Stick with it, even though initial attendance may not be as full as you'd hoped. Set your time horizon to years, not just weeks or months. Above all, pray that the Lord would make your congregation more faithful to gather for corporate prayer. The Lord loves to answer that one.

Think Tank

1. Why might it not be best to use the adult education hour for age-graded teaching and fellowship?

2. Why, biblically, might we avoid using the Sunday morning service primarily for evangelism?

3. Why be intentional about making the Sunday evening service different from the morning service?

Wednesday Evening Service

The Wednesday evening service is the main *study* time. Ministry philosophies vary widely regarding the use of the midweek service, or even whether to have one at all. When we started our Wednesday evening service, not very many people came. But over the years, as people benefited from the teaching of Scripture, word spread and attendance became more encouraging and steady. We have benefited greatly from using this as a time for the whole church to gather for inductive Bible study. How in the world does *that* work?

We always study an epistle on Wednesday nights, since the New Testament letters lend themselves particularly well to the inductive method (observation, interpretation, and application). We take it slow—a verse or two per week, usually investing a few years in the same book. This may seem tedious, but it gives the whole congregation the opportunity to wrestle through important doctrines together, to figure out as a church how they apply to us both individually and corporately, and to evaluate ourselves together as to whether or not we're really obeying this part of Scripture as a church.

Usually, I'll start by reading a portion of a good Christian book by a solidly evangelical author. I'll run through some very brief announcements, pray, and then read the surrounding passage of the verse or two that we plan to study that night. Our little passage for study will be written on a dry-erase board, and I'll just start asking questions: first about what the text says (observation), then about what the text means (interpretation), and finally about what it means for us (application).

Observation questions might include the following: What does Paul say to do here? How does he say to do it? What does he say will happen? When will that happen? Who is Paul talking about here? Why does he say this, according to the context? Sometimes these starter questions are obvious, but asking them models responsible Bible study for the congregation and helps to ensure that we apply the text correctly. Interpretation questions might include: What does it mean to "pray always"? What does it not mean? Might it have an intended double meaning that would make sense in context? Application questions then move toward asking things like: Do you do this? How? When you don't apply this passage, what is it that keeps you from doing so? Are we doing this faithfully as a congregation? How could we be doing it better? Are there ways that we need to stop applying this passage because we've misunderstood it?

When I first started doing this, I sometimes had to wait through thirty (or even sixty!) seconds of silence before someone would raise their hand to offer an answer. But now that the congregation has gotten used to the idea and has had a few years of practice at it, those silences are both shorter and much less frequent. I say this as an encouragement! Don't let a fear of silence keep you from stepping out in faith and leading a large group Bible study like this! The silence won't last forever! Someone will eventually speak up. If they don't, just calmly rephrase the question or casually ask a more mature and articulate member of the congregation to share his thoughts. As people get more practice at thinking through things together like that, they will become more comfortable with speaking up, and the conversation will become more lively and productive. You may just need to be patient with the congregation while they adapt.

Whatever the case, make sure you yourself have studied the passage closely so that you will be able to answer reasonable questions. You'll probably have to say "I don't know" in some cases—I know I do. But that's okay. No one expects you to be omniscient (and if they do, they're being unreasonable). Besides, it's good for your humility to say "I don't know" in public every once in a while.

Think Tank

1. Think of three ways a weekly, large group, inductive Bible study might benefit your church.

Members' Meetings

Members' meetings are the main *administrative* times. More commonly known as business meetings, members' meetings are so much more of a privilege than we often give them credit for! We are meeting together to conduct the affairs of the kingdom as the church grows and expands—there is scarcely anything more important that we could be doing! So how do you conduct a members' meeting in a way that doesn't lead to carnal disagreement?

The first step goes all the way back to how you take in new members. Make sure that, as far as you can tell, every person who becomes a member of your church is actually converted (see chap. 4)! Unbelievers who participate in church business meetings will only ever do so with a carnal, selfish, prideful heart—they've never been given a new one. It only makes sense, then, that their participation in these meetings could too often be less than helpful or charitable.

The second step is to gather around you some elder-qualified men who can give you wisdom about what issues to handle when, and who can help you say things in a more gentle, more charitable, and less harsh or defensive way. Running your agenda and your planned statements by a group of godly, wise, and biblically informed and governed men can keep you from saying unhelpful things in unhelpful ways at unhelpful times.

Another important measure to take is to distribute the agenda a week in advance so that people can look it over, pray through it, and even air their concerns with you or the chairman in private so that the public meeting is not peppered with thoughtless, divisive, or combative questions. Giving people some time to think about the issues and even approach the pastors in private helps to remove the shock factor often inherent in business meetings.

If you do have elders, make sure they are all on the same page regarding each issue on the agenda so that members can talk to any one of them and get the same basic answer. One of the most helpful things we've done is to have a meeting of all the elders a week in advance of every members' meeting in order to ensure unity and good communication among the leaders. It simply is not good for weaker sheep to see their leaders question each other in the middle of a business meeting. Unity among the congregation will more likely be achieved if they see that the leaders they've previously recognized are already in harmony respecting the motions brought before the congregation. Such prior preparation can also serve as a preventative measure, discouraging less mature members from sowing seeds of division.

Having elders may also mean that one of these men may actually be better at leading those members' meetings than you are. I (and others!) noticed that I tended to get defensive sometimes when certain questions were asked at members' meetings. So now they are led by another elder whose gifts, personality, and demeanor lend themselves much more naturally to the role. That decision made a difference in how smoothly those meetings go, and I praise God for the gift of having other godly leaders to complement my strengths and weaknesses.

One of the most important things that happens in a members' meeting at our church is the introduction of prospective members. These people won't actually attend the meeting, since we haven't yet voted them into membership. But as the pastor, I will put a picture of the person on an overhead projector and briefly (in one to two minutes) recount the person's testimony in order to give the congregation an idea of who it is that they are voting to accept as a member. This practice gives the congregation an opportunity to evaluate the person's testimony themselves and notifies them of who the new members are so that they can begin to form relationships with them. It also serves as a not-so-subtle reminder to the congregation of the importance of their role in taking in new members in a deliberate, responsible, and well-informed way.

Some of the other things that should be addressed in members' meetings include a finance report since the last meeting, ministry reports from different departments, an elders' report regarding the nomination of new elders or deacons, updates on missionaries, updates on physical facilities issues, "seeing out" those who have removed their membership, or taking corporate action on discipline cases.[3]

Members' meetings can change from being about dull and routine business to being times of honest discussion and encouragement, sobering discipline, and exciting vision building. By God's grace, that change has happened in our congregation.

11

The Role of the Ordinances

OFTEN AS EVANGELICALS, the thing we emphasize most about the ordinances is that they're not necessary for salvation. Beyond this, we are sometimes reticent to put forward a positive view of the role of the ordinances. So what is the place of the ordinances in the local church, and how do they contribute to its corporate health and holiness?

Baptism

According to the Bible, baptism is fundamentally a physical sign of a spiritual reality. Matthew 28:18–20 indicates that it is for believers only, the initial step of obedience in our new life of discipleship to Christ. Romans 6:1–4 is even more specific, indicating that baptism symbolizes our death and burial with Christ as our representative head, and our spiritual resurrection with him from the symbolic grave. Colossians 2:11–13 indicates even more specifically still that baptism is the physical representation of the spiritual circumcision of our hearts.[1] As such, it functions as something of an identity marker, initially identifying us as members of the new covenant—those who have received new hearts from God (Ezek. 36:26–27). In other words, baptism identifies us as members of the community called the people of God—the church.

Baptism, then, is the ordinance that guards the front door of the local church. It ensures, as far as externally possible, that those who become members of our churches really are members of the new covenant, complete with new hearts. In requiring every member to be baptized as a believer, we are only asking them to obey the first commandment Jesus gives his disciples—to externally identify ourselves with his people (Matt. 28:19)—thus verifying their discipleship to him. This is the primary way that we protect the *regeneracy* of church membership. That is, by being baptized as a believer, each potential new member is publicly stating that his heart has been circumcised by the Spirit, that he has been crucified, buried, and raised with Christ. He is testifying by his own symbolic actions that he has in fact genuinely repented and believed in the gospel. In so doing, he identifies himself as one whose heart has truly been *regenerated*—a new creation in Christ, and as such a member of God's people.

If baptism functions as guardian of the front door of the local church, then baptizing children may actually endanger regenerate church membership and therefore the purity of the church's corporate testimony in the community. By God's design, children are naturally malleable to the instruction and example of their parents. If we baptize them prematurely, then we risk affirming a profession that was made simply to please believing parents or to be accepted by a Christian subculture, thus perpetuating nominalism (albeit unwittingly).[2] Waiting to baptize the young until they've reached their majority helps to ensure that we do not wrongly affirm a spurious profession with the sign of baptism.[3]

When we have baptisms at our church, we place them at the end of the morning service because that is when the maximum number of members and visitors will be present to observe. I first introduce the candidates to the congregation and then ask them to give a brief (three-minute) testimony of how they were converted and why they want to be baptized as believers. I then ask them two questions:

Do you make profession of repentance toward God and of faith in the Lord Jesus Christ?

Do you promise, by God's grace, to follow him forever in the fellowship of his church?

After they answer in the affirmative, the candidate(s) and I prepare to enter the baptistery as the congregation sings a hymn. Once we're in the water, I say, "John, upon your profession of repentance toward God and faith in the Lord Jesus Christ, I baptize you in the name of the Father, the Son, and the Holy Spirit."

Think Tank

1. What is the biblical role of baptism? Does it play this role in your church? Why or why not?

The Lord's Supper

According to Paul in 1 Corinthians 11:17–34, the Lord's Supper is several things all wrapped into one. It is first an opportunity to express the unity of the church (vv. 18–19, 33). It is therefore, second, a fellowship of God's people (vv. 20–21, 33). Third, it is intended as a symbolic remembrance of Christ's sinless life and atoning death on our behalf (vv. 24–25). Fourth, it is intended as a proclamation of Christ's death, resurrection, and return (v. 26). And fifth, it is a built-in opportunity for self-examination (vv. 28–29). Taking the Lord's Supper, then, is a participation in the unity of the church's fellowship around the remembrance of Jesus Christ and the proclamation of his saving person and work through the symbols of bread and wine.

At our church, we begin the observation of the Lord's Supper by silently reflecting on the church covenant as a means by which to examine our own hearts. We then renew our covenant by standing and reading it aloud together, after which we distribute the elements. We take the bread individually to symbolize our individual discipleship to Christ, and we hold the cup until all have been served in order to take it together as a symbol of our corporate unity in Christ.

As baptism guards the front door of the church, the Lord's Supper takes its post at the back door. Communion is a symbol of the unity and fellowship of the church. The prerequisites for participation in that symbol are continued repentance and belief. It follows, then, that those who do not meet the prerequisites of unity with the church should be excluded from participation in the symbol of that unity. Those giving either no evidence or contrary evidence regarding genuine repentance and belief should be excluded from the Lord's Supper. In barring an unrepentant member from the Lord's Table, we are treating him as an unbelieving outsider. That is, we are barring him from the primary symbol of church unity and fellowship, and thereby clarifying the boundary between the church and the world.[4] Participation in the Lord's Supper clarifies that a person remains in the church and enjoys this privilege of membership. Exclusion from the Lord's Supper clarifies that a person has forfeited this privilege and escorts him out of church membership.[5]

Think Tank

1. What is the biblical role of the Lord's Supper? Does it play this role in your church? Why or why not?

Conclusion

Both ordinances, baptism and the Lord's Supper, serve as symbolic identity markers that clarify which people are members of the church. Baptism is our initial symbolic act of obedience that identifies us as disciples, protecting the regeneracy of church membership as we enter the front door of the church. Participation in the Lord's Supper is a continuing symbolic act of unity and fellowship in Christ that identifies us as those who are continuing members of the church in good standing. Exclusion from the Lord's Supper identifies those who have either given no evidence or have given contrary evidence regarding their own repentance and belief, and thus have been escorted out of church membership.

12

Loving Each Other

JESUS TOLD THE TWELVE that the world would know that they were his disciples by their love for one another (John 13:34–35). The same goes for the church. Selfless, humble, Christlike love is to be the signature of those who claim to be members of the local church. Showing distinctively Christian love for one another, then, is a critical evangelistic tool for the spread of the gospel and the growth of the church. What this means for the pastor and church leader, however, is that we need to be deliberately cultivating a culture of Christian love and concern in order that the local church would be known as a genuine, distinctively Christian community in the surrounding neighborhood.

The cultivation of this kind of loving Christian community is what we have been working toward in chapters 1–11. The goal of gathering the church and ordering our weekly gatherings is to cultivate a culture that has evangelistic effects on our unbelieving friends. In this chapter, we'll take a look at a few of the contours of that culture.

A Live, Active Culture

I always thought it a bit odd that the makers of yogurt would try to sell their product by pointing out that it has "live, active cultures"! It has never stopped me from eating it. But every time I read that phrase before enjoying a refreshing yogurt experience, I half wonder if the little guys might try to crawl back out of my mouth!

Hopefully this little reflection hasn't ruined *your* next yogurt experience. Regardless, the church is to be full of live, active cultures—relationships that are mutually encouraging and help people grow spiritually. Churches should be full of spiritually dynamic friendships in which older Christians are helping to teach and guide younger Christians in the Word, where peers get together regularly for accountability and prayer, and where Christians are reading nourishing Christian books together and talking about how they can use them to grow spiritually. This live, active culture of love has at least five different aspects. You may be able to think of more.

Covenantal. The first aspect of any local church community is that it is covenantal. That is, it is a community of believers who have become part of the new covenant in Christ's blood and, as a result, have covenanted together to help each other run the Christian race with integrity, godliness, and grace. It is a community of mutual commitment to doing each other good spiritually—bearing each other's burdens, sharing joys, giving to support the ministry, exercising affectionate watchfulness over one another, and at times rebuking the unrepentant or submitting to correction ourselves as occasion may require. In signing a church covenant (see chap. 4), we are committing to grasp hold of one another in Christian love and accountability, and to submit ourselves to both the encouragement and the correction of our fellow believers.

Think Tank

1. Read Ephesians 4:15–16. How does the body grow? Why are relationships important to this growth?

2. Read Hebrews 10:24–25. Why do we gather together? Why are relationships important for this purpose?

3. How might a church covenant be useful for building each other up spiritually?

Careful. The church's culture of mutual love should also be marked by a carefulness—a deliberateness—that shows our concern for obeying God's Word in every aspect of our corporate life together. We want to show intentionality at every step—not simply that we have good intentions, but that everything we do is deliberately planned to serve the functional centrality of the gospel.

Corporate. In cultivating a culture of mutual love, we want to make sure we encourage people to place a high priority on the corporate life of the congregation, not simply on their own individual walks with the Lord. The nature of the Christian life is corporate, because the body of Christ is a corporate entity. While our individual walks are crucial, we are impoverished in our personal pursuit of God if we do not avail ourselves of the help that is available through mutually edifying relationships in our covenant church family (Eph. 4:15–16; Heb. 10:24–25).

We can encourage members to prioritize the corporate life of the church by teaching them about the biblical place of the church in the life of the believer, praying for them, encouraging them to attend services more than simply once a week, expecting their attendance at members' meetings, encouraging them to make known their desires to serve as deacons of our church's different ministries, encouraging them to pray through the membership directory a page at a time, and challenging them to serve in an area for which they may not necessarily feel ideally equipped. Cultivating the priority of the local congregation in the lives of individual members will help curb our selfish individualism and create an atmosphere of humble servanthood.

But again, they must be taught from the Bible that the corporate life of the congregation should be central to the life of the individual believer (John 13:34–35; Eph. 3:10–11; 4:11–16; Heb. 10:24–25; 1 John 4:20–21). We can't live the Christian life alone. We are saved individually from our sins, yet we are not saved into a vacuum. We're saved into a mutually edifying community of believers who are building each other up and spurring each other on to love and good deeds.

Cross-cultural. The local church is for everyone. That's why it is difficult to defend the practice of targeting a church to a particular demographic based on any factor other than language. Targeted churches can have the unintended effect of obscuring the transcultural, unifying power of the gospel. When the gospel enables us to live in love, even though we may have nothing else in common save Christ, it is a testimony to its power to transform a group of sinful, self-centered people into a loving community united by a common relationship with Jesus Christ.

Cross-generational. The local church is a family. It's a place where children and adults of all ages can and should be relating to one another for mutual encouragement and edification. Older Christian men often have much to teach younger men about life and leadership, and there are countless ways that younger men can serve and help the elderly. Older Christian women often have much to teach younger women about serving in the home and church, and younger women can often serve older women in countless ways, whether it be social, spiritual, or physical. Young singles can serve in the nursery or teach children's Sunday school, developing parenting skills for themselves and encouraging young children in the faith.

We've experienced the power of cross-generational fellowship as an evangelistic witness. Visitors wonder why so many young people are at an older member's funeral or how that widow has so many young people coming to her house to lend her a hand. The point is that, in the context of a niche-marketed society, the church can stand out as a unique beacon in the community for being a web of warm cross-generational relationships that are grounded in the gospel.

Building a Corporate Witness

The ultimate goal of building this kind of community—one built on distinctively Christian love that flows from the distinctively Christian gospel—is to display God's glory throughout our surrounding neighborhoods, our cities, and ultimately the world. We're right back at John 13:34–35: "A new commandment I give to you, that you love one another, even as I have loved you, that you also love one another. By this all men will know that you are My disciples, if you have love for one another." Our Christlike love for one another is intended by God to be the church's most powerful tool for evangelism!

This is the reason that depending on a *program* for evangelistic effectiveness is a little like outsourcing the main responsibility of the church. Evangelism programs are not necessarily or categorically bad. Some are quite good. But I fear we sometimes depend on them so much that we forget that the *church itself* is God's evangelism program. The mutually loving relationships in the church are designed by God to be attractive to an unbelieving culture. The covenantal, careful, corporate, cross-cultural, and cross-generational love that is to characterize the church and glorify God is at the same time intended to evangelize the world.

Conclusion

Internalizing and applying these biblical truths will make all the difference in how we go about building a local church body. Instead of wrongly affirming the priority of the individual over that of the corporate whole, we will teach people that growing in love for one another and in concern for the corporate good of the church is pivotal to the growth and health of the body. Instead of relying on programs, we'll disciple people. Instead of relying on paid staff members to do all the ministry, we'll teach people by both word and deed to initiate personal conversations and relationships with other members of the church in order to do them good spiritually. Instead of looking for the next man-made ministry model to make our church a success, we'll entrust ourselves to the transforming power of the gospel to change our hearts and build a community of Christians characterized by selfless love and genuine concern for others. Being deliberate makes a difference.

13

Music

NOW WHY WOULD WE HAVE a whole chapter titled "Music"? Isn't that a little whimsical? Why not be more sanctified and call it "Worship"? After all, it's common today to speak of music, singing, and worship as interchangeable things. First we worship, then we listen to the sermon.

We want to challenge this assumption. Music in the context of the corporate gathering is only a subset of corporate worship. Listening to the preached Word of God is one of the most important ways we worship God together; in fact, it is the only way we can learn how to worship him acceptably.[1] Praying the Word, reading it publicly, and seeing it in the ordinances are also important aspects of worship. Yet more broadly, worship is a total life orientation of engaging with God on the terms that he proposes and in the way that he provides.[2] Our reasonable service of New Testament worship is to present *our whole selves* as living sacrifices, holy and acceptable to God (Rom. 12:1–2; cf. 1 Cor. 10:31; Col. 3:17). So music is a subset of our corporate worship, and corporate worship is a subset of our total-life worship.

This reflection reminds us that our audience in corporate worship is not people.[3] Corporate worship is not about pleasing or entertaining people, whether ourselves, the congregation, or unbelieving seekers. Worship in the corporate gathering is about renewing our covenant with God by meeting with him and relating to him in the ways that he has prescribed.[4] We do this specifically by hearing and heeding his Word, confessing our own sinfulness and our dependence on him, thanking him for his goodness to us, bringing our requests before him, confessing his truth, and lifting our voices and instruments to him in response to and in accord with the way that he has revealed himself in his Word.[5]

Against that backdrop, here are some practical suggestions that might help us glorify God and edify one another in corporate musical worship.

Congregational Singing

Singing the gospel together as a whole church forges unity around distinctively Christian doctrine and practice. Our congregational songs function like devotional creeds. They give us language and opportunity to mutually encourage each other in the Word and call each other out to praise our common Savior. One of the most important functions of congregational singing is that it highlights the *corporate* nature of the church and the mutual ministry that builds us up in unity. One reason we come together on Sundays is to remind ourselves that we are not alone in our confession of Jesus Christ and our conviction of the spiritual truths we hold so dearly. What a blessing it is to hear the whole church singing together with all our hearts! When we hear one another singing the same words all together, there is both a common melody and a diverse harmony that expresses the unity and diversity of the local church body in a way that encourages us to press on together. In our overly individualized culture, congregational singing is one of the most visible ways to encourage a specifically corporate emphasis to our worship and life as a local church body.

Another important function of congregational singing is that it highlights the *participative* nature of musical worship. Worship in general is not something we can do as spectators. Romans 12:1–2 portrays worship as active. It is also suggestive to note that we have no example of a church choir in the New Testament—the Bible never represents first-century believers entering into musical worship vicariously through the singing of another group or individual. Rather, the musical worship is participatory—the whole congregation corporately participates in worshiping God with one heart and voice. The Bible certainly calls us to listen to and respond to God's Word. But this kind of listening is a particular response to a biblically commanded method of communication—preaching. When it comes to musical worship, the Bible presents believers engaging in worship themselves, all together. This is not to say, of course, that solos and special music are necessarily wrong. Nor is it to deny that solos and special music can be spiritually moving to those who hear them. The issue is simply what kind of corporate musical worship we see modeled in the New Testament church, and what we say about corporate musical worship if many of our songs are performed by a few rather than participated in by all.

A steady diet of performances by soloists or even choirs can have the unintended effect of undermining the corporate, participative nature of our musical worship. People can gradually come to think of worship in terms of passive observation, which we do not see modeled in the Bible. Such a diet may also begin to blur the line between worship and entertainment, especially in a television-saturated culture, where one of our most insidious expectations is to be always entertained. Of course, this blurring is hardly ever intended. But over time, separating the "performers" from "the rest of the congregation" can subtly shift the focus of our attention from God to the musicians and their talent—a shift that is frequently revealed by applause at the end of some performance pieces. Who is the beneficiary of such applause?

If what we're doing on Sunday mornings is *corporate* worship, then it makes sense to give deliberate preference to *congregational* singing—singing that involves the active participation of the *whole* congregation.

When we sing God's praises *together*, we are recognizing the corporate nature of the church's confessional life. That is, we are corporately affirming that we confess Christian doctrine and experience the Christian life *together* with our covenant community. Congregational singing, then, is true to both the corporate and the participatory aspects of our regular corporate worship. It steers clear of the entertainment trap precisely by involving the whole people of God in the active praise of God, responding vocally to his goodness and grace with audible praise and thanksgiving.

Now that we have briefly suggested congregational singing as an implication of corporate musical worship, it might be helpful to remember three guidelines for congregational singing.

It is public, not privatized. Many musical worship leaders encourage members (by either word or deed) to close their eyes in pursuit of private emotional intimacy with God in the context of the corporate gathering. Now, no one in his right mind would argue that closing one's eyes in corporate worship is categorically wrong. And many close their eyes in the corporate gathering simply to take in the sound of the singing more fully. But we would be wrong to encourage people to think of corporate worship in terms of shutting out the rest of the congregation to have a privatized emotional experience with God.[6]

I was once in a service where the music leader started crying uncontrollably on the platform after leading a song. Was this a healthy model of brokenness? Perhaps, and I have no doubt that he intended it as such. The purity of his heart is not at issue. It is the wisdom of his public demeanor that I would question. He was teaching people by example that privatized emotional experience, even though released in front of the whole congregation, is the ultimate expression of (corporate) worship. That simply isn't true.

Congregational singing is an expression of the unity and harmony of the gathered congregation. Privatizing corporate worship, then, defeats the purpose of corporate worship and often confuses true worship with privatized emotion. The corporate worship gathering is a public meeting; we are intended to experience it aware of our togetherness. Much of the edifying power of congregational singing actually comes from enjoying the presence of our fellow worshipers. Why else would we come together in song if this weren't the case? It is best, then, not to privatize what God has decreed should be public.

It should be theologically rich. God has given us so much to be encouraged about in his Word! We should use the rich storehouse of Scripture to give us good things to say in our praise of him, to remind us of the perfections of God's character and the sufficiency of Christ's work. We want to sing songs that raise our view of God, that present him in all his glory and grace. We want to sing songs that put the details of Christ's person and work front and center. We want to sing theologically textured songs that make us think about the depths of God's character, the contours of his grace, and the implications of his gospel; that teach us about the biblical doctrine that saves and transforms. Negatively, we want to avoid songs that encourage us to reflect on our own subjective emotional experience more than on the objective truths of God's character and implications of the cross. We also want to avoid needless repetition of phrases in almost mantralike fashion, as if seeking an emotional high were the purest form of worship.

Examine the following lyrics:

Who is He in yonder stall,
At whose feet the shepherds fall?
Who is He in deep distress,
Fasting in the wilderness?

Chorus:
'Tis the Lord! O wondrous story!
'Tis the Lord! The King of glory!

At His feet we humbly fall,
Crown Him! Crown Him, Lord of all!

Who is He the people bless
For His words of gentleness?
Who is He to whom they bring
All the sick and sorrowing? (*Chorus*)

Who is He that stands and weeps
At the grave where Laz'rus sleeps?
Who is He the gathering throng
Greet with loud triumphant song? (*Chorus*)

Lo! At midnight, who is He
Prays in dark Gethsemane?
Who is He on yonder tree
Dies in grief and agony? (*Chorus*)

Who is He that from the grave
Comes to heal and help and save?
Who is He that from His throne
Rules thro' all the world alone? (*Chorus*)[7]

This hymn includes only one first-person reference. But it is in the plural—we—and it has to do with us worshiping God and recognizing his kingship.[8] The whole hymn is centered on God in Christ. And notice the sense of movement or progression—the lyrics take us from Christ's manger to his throne. It's a musical, meditative history of the life of Christ that draws us out to worship him as he is presented in the Bible. And the music is meditative, complementing the reverent nature of the lyrics. These are the hallmarks of good worship songs, whether they're hymns or choruses: biblical accuracy, God centeredness, theological and/or historical progression, absence of first-person singular pronouns, and music that complements the tone of the lyrics.

It should be spiritually encouraging. The result of theological richness will always be increasing accuracy in worshiping God as he really is, which will in turn result in increasing spiritual encouragement for us. Our hope is in the character of God and the truth of his gospel! In corporate musical worship, we are calling out to each other to praise God for his glorious character and works. We are giving audible expression to the unity and harmony of the church, and to the corporate nature of confessional Christian life.[9] We are encouraging each other, by the strength of our voices, that we are not alone in our confession, but that everyone else who is singing is affirming the truth and significance of the words being sung. The more, the merrier! This kind of congregational singing is a powerful encouragement to our souls, reminding us of our fellowship and unity in the truths that we sing. What we want to encourage, then, is a marked priority and emphasis on the congregation actually singing together, both in unity and in harmony, so that God is honored by our active corporate participation in musical worship, and so that we can hear each other and be edified ourselves.

Think Tank

1. What makes congregational singing particularly well-suited to the corporate worship gathering?

2. How might a steady diet of performed worship music affect a local church negatively?

3. Is performed music more valued than congregational singing in your church? If so, why?

4. How might the three guidelines for corporate worship music apply to your own church?

Accompaniment

What about musical accompaniment for our corporate singing? These can sometimes be choppy waters to navigate. Often pastors try to please everyone with the musical style and end up pleasing no one. Some pastors try to gear the music to the expectations of unbelieving listeners. Some pay too little attention to the accompaniment, thinking that since it's not a "salvation issue," it's altogether unimportant. Here are a few guidelines for congregational singing that we've observed with great encouragement and profit.

Music serves lyrics. It simply doesn't make sense to sing songs if the lyrics are saying one thing and the music is saying another. So we need to start with the understanding that music is designed to complement lyrics, not contradict them. Joyful lyrics should be put to joyful music, and mournful lyrics should be put to mournful music. The musical accompaniment should not be chosen on the basis of pleasing the most people or suiting the tastes of either members or seekers. Musical accompaniment should be chosen primarily based on what kind of music reinforces the intention and message of different kinds of biblical lyrics and poetry.

Triumphalism is premature. Most of us have heard songs of total victory that finish with a high note and an instrumental flourish, often right before the sermon. There's certainly nothing morally wrong with hitting high notes. But it's the triumphalistic attitude of some songs—the idea that all our battles are over and it's time to enjoy complete victory over all our spiritual enemies—that is as yet premature in these last days. Such triumphalism in our music is particularly ill suited as preparation for listening to a Christian sermon. In the sermon, we are about to hear God's Word correct, instruct, rebuke, warn, and, yes, also encourage, warm, and delight our hearts. Meditative music serves us much better in preparing our hearts to hear and heed God's Word.[10]

We still have much work to do in the field of God's harvest. Many battles lie ahead. The church is not yet the church victorious—she is still the church militant. Joy, gladness, contentment, love, and a host of other positive sentiments are rightly expressed. But our music should not contradict our location in the history of God's saving work. The kingdom has only been inaugurated. It has yet to fully come. Our music should show an appropriate restraint.

Simple is best. There's certainly nothing wrong with electric guitars or a driving backbeat, and there are plenty of contemporary examples of churches and worship bands that are faithfully wedding popular music with theologically accurate lyrics. We are persuaded, though, that sparse, lightly amplified instrumentation and unobtrusive leaders are best for the weekly corporate worship gathering. The main reason is that quieter instrumentation allows the congregation to hear themselves singing, giving the lyrics center stage and encouraging the congregation to sing all the louder. Fewer instruments on stage or even off to the side means fewer things in front of us competing for our attention and applause. The presence of a fully wired worship band may not necessarily bring an atmosphere of performance to the meeting. But the absence of a fully wired worship band will help prevent the smog of performance from clouding the atmosphere of worship. We use a piano, a guitar, and four vocalists, all positioned off to the side so that our attention isn't drawn to them, and all lightly amplified so that they don't drown out the voices of the congregation. This simplicity in instrumentation also helps to maintain a spirit of unity when there is a diversity of musical tastes and opinions represented in a congregation.

Again, we would be foolish to argue that electrical instruments and fully wired worship bands are categorically wrong or even necessarily distracting. But in refraining from heavy instrumentation and even from heavy dependence on electrical amplification, we protect ourselves and others from dependence on these things as necessities for corporate musical worship. This instrumental sparseness is simply another way that we keep our methods basic so that the gospel remains clearly at the center even of how we worship in song. As a result, it also becomes a more replicable model for deployment by smaller church plants.

One of the musical practices that ironically encourages congregational participation is actually singing a verse of a song or hymn a cappella—yes, actually without instrumental accompaniment of any kind! This seems counterintuitive at first. The common wisdom is that more accompaniment will encourage a kind of "safe space" for unskilled singers. And many Christians see warrant for such an approach in Psalm 98:5–6.

But the center of heaven's worship in Revelation is not instrumentation; it's verbal articulation in song. And we're commanded in the Epistles to speak to one another in psalms, hymns, and spiritual songs (Eph. 5:19; Col. 3:16). From a practical perspective, have you ever considered that more instrumental noise often only functions as an excuse to observe an unwitting concert rather than participate in congregational worship? Whereas if you encourage the singing of four-part harmony with a lightly amplified vocal quartet and a piano player who plays just the four parts so the congregation can follow them, you might be surprised at how emboldened a congregation's singing can become.

So when you decide to go a capella, do it on songs with four-part harmony. This is a good way to give the congregation more to do in the service. It also makes a capella singing sound better, which then encourages even more congregational participation. And rest assured, making the musical parts available to the congregation by printing the sheet music in the bulletin is always a good use of paper![11]

In all this, it's important to recognize that songs don't just teach doctrine (Col. 3:16), they make it stick with a melodic adhesive that can hold for a lifetime. This means selecting congregational songs and hymns is one of the most crucial aspects of the pastor's job. If you as the main preaching pastor don't feel musically qualified to pick music, then choose another elder who can do this important work. Regardless, we are all far more likely to quote a hymn than a sermon on our deathbed, so make sure the songs you're singing together are the ones you want to hear ringing in your soul as you cross that farther shore.

Leaders are self-effacing. Many of us have been in churches where the music leader uses flamboyant hand motions, body language, or even facial expressions. Vocalists who are intentionally self-effacing serve the congregation well by taking themselves out of the spotlight so that our attention is not directed toward them. They may do this by saying fewer things, minimizing gestures, positioning themselves to the side, or even stepping down off the platform altogether. Our leading vocalists simply stand to the side and sing into moderately amplified microphones so that there is a strong lead for the congregation to follow.

Variety—a Staple Spice

Healthy churches avoid worship wars. They even avoid worship skirmishes. Wise church leaders know that using a wide variety of songs and styles over time broadens a congregation's tastes, exposing them to different kinds of music from different time periods and cultivating in them at least a modest level of appreciation for the best selections from each. Conversely, variety in worship songs and styles helps prevent people from becoming militantly entrenched in a certain style or period of music. Best of all, musical variety teaches us to glean spiritual profit from many different kinds of songs. Here are some operating categories.

Hymns and praise choruses. Let's all just be honest and admit that we can find really good and really bad examples of both. Wisdom, then, is not to choose one category over the other, but to cull the best from both genres and intermingle them in each service.

Major and minor keys. We shouldn't limit ourselves to major key songs! The Psalms reveal that much of the Christian life might be spent in a minor key, and it's time that the church became honest about this reality as well. The church needs to be able to lament together, and minor key songs help us do that. They help us to be honest about the trials and emotions that we encounter on our pilgrimage to heaven. They help give expression to our sorrowful thoughts and feelings in ways that honor God and encourage us to persevere. We neglect them to our own impoverishment.[12]

A variety of sources. Let's not limit ourselves to the hymnal we found in the pews when we first arrived at our church. There are plenty of solid music resources out there that can broaden the scope of our musical repertoire. Here are a few we find most useful:

- *Hymns of Grace* (Los Angeles: The Master's Seminary Press, 2015)
- *Trinity Hymnal* (Suwanee, GA: Great Commission Publications, 1990)
- *African American Heritage Hymnal: 575 Hymns, Spirituals, and Gospel Songs* (Chicago: GIA Publications, 2001)
- *Grace Hymns* (London: Grace Publications Trust, 1984)

Placement. The most intuitive way to decide "what to sing when" is to think about what you're preaching on and then go to the topical index in the hymnal or praise book to see what songs fit. But this is precisely the reason that we keep singing the same songs all the time! We all have favorites in every category, so our attention is always drawn to those.

Try this. Instead of deciding the intuitive way, deliberately commit to working your way through the pew hymnal and a few other resources every year or two. January through March, you go through hymns 1–100; April through June, hymns 101–200; and so on through the year, adding other sources as you acquire them. Pick the theologically accurate songs from those sections of the songbook that you maybe haven't sung for a while, and then match those songs to the theological themes of the services you're planning for that part of the year.

As you can see, this takes quite a bit of forethought and planning on your part. Then again, it's difficult to become a deliberate church without being, well, deliberate.

Getting There

Of course, if you're a young pastor just entering a reforming situation, the music situation will not likely be ideal—perhaps not even in the vicinity of ideal. That's okay. Don't try to change all the music all at once. Youth is often the mother of impatience, and a young, highly motivated, strongly convicted pastor might be tempted to drive 85 miles per hour in a church with a speed limit of 30. Many congregations simply don't know that much music. Most churches are also on the smaller side, so they don't generate much vocal volume; and some aren't very skilled musically. So if you plan your Sunday service using a bunch of songs that no one knows, it won't be encouraging to anyone—no matter how biblical the lyrics are. People won't sing with confidence, so it will sound timid, which will end up having a discouraging and maybe even an alienating effect.

Start with what *they* know, not with what you know. Begin by building their musical confidence on songs they're familiar with. If the church is full of older people, chances are they'll know some of the old hymns that have sound lyrics and singable melodies. Sing those. Also, look through their music selection and find some choruses that say some biblical things about God's character, our sin, and Christ's person and work. They may not have today's most biblical choruses, but that's okay. Just dig out the best ones and work with what they've got. It will speak volumes to them of your humility and patience if you meet them where they are and start from there.

As you plan the music, think about making gradual progress on two axes—the skill axis and the knowledge axis (see Fig. 12.1). Depending on the skill level of your congregation, try teaching them a new song or two every month. Start with songs that are easy to sing—not too many dipsy-doos. When you introduce a song for the first time, maybe have the pianist play the tune once through so that people can hear the melody before they try to sing it. It may also be a good idea to place a brand-new song in a position of the service that follows the singing of a few well-known songs. This can build the congregation's musical confidence so that they feel warmed up and ready to learn a new one. Also, once you've sung a new song for the first time as a congregation, consider bringing it back out the very next week so that people can practice it again and become more familiar with it. Sing it two or three weeks in a row, and then retire it for a while in the "We know this one" pile. Even if you teach only one or two new songs every month, you'll have learned between twelve and twenty-four new songs as a congregation that year. That's great!

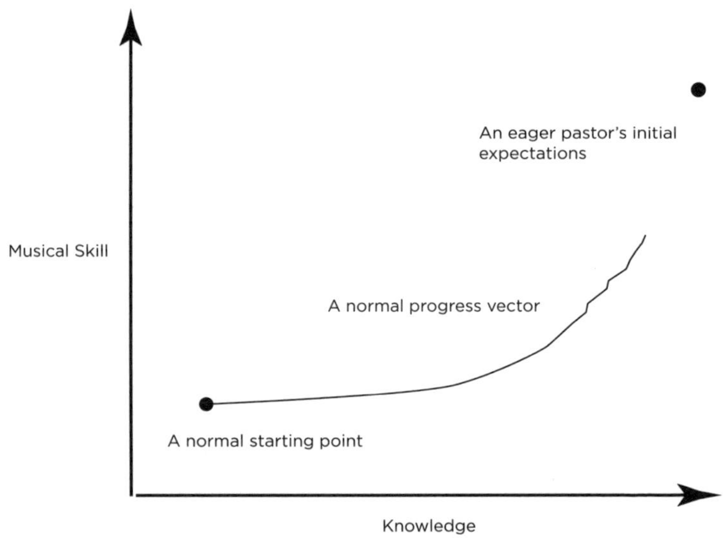

Figure 13.1—Musical Progress Grid for a Normal Congregation

As you continue to teach over the years, you may find that you don't have a lot of musically gifted people in your congregation. That's okay. Growth in the number of songs known will usually outpace growth of the congregation's musical skill level, at least at the outset. Just keep teaching them songs with singable tunes and solid lyrics. Keep expanding their knowledge base, and be gentle and understanding with respect to their limited ability to sing more difficult tunes. Challenge, but don't discourage.

Think Tank

1. How might your church benefit from a wider variety of worship music?

2. How can an intentionally sparse musical accompaniment enhance congregational singing?

3. Are your music leaders self-effacing? Or do they attract attention to themselves?

Conclusion

We've been thinking about what to do when the church gathers. As we've seen, everything that happens up front in the corporate gatherings of the church is part of the teaching ministry of the church. Scripture regulates the church's teaching. Accordingly, every element of the main weekly gathering should have positive warrant from Scripture, either in the form of a clear command or a good and necessary consequence of a particular passage. This may seem constrictive at first. But in the long run it will actually liberate you from the tyranny of the latest innovation or the most popular fad—what we might conveniently refer to as the tyranny of the new.

We, as pastors and church leaders, will lead our congregations to think of corporate worship in a particular way simply by how we structure and lead it. An important aim of the deliberate church is to make sure that everything that happens up front is deliberately faithful to the intention of Scripture and good for the health and growth of the church. The implication, then, is that the pastor, as the primary biblical teacher and preacher recognized by the church, is finally responsible for everything that is preached, prayed, read, sung, and seen in the public worship gatherings. This being the case, the pastor is the one who is ultimately responsible for being deliberate in deciding what makes the cut and what does not.

Being deliberate about our weekly gatherings, especially about the main weekly worship gathering, takes a lot of work. In particular, it takes planning out Sunday services weeks and even months ahead of time, instead of operating week to week. This may seem intimidating at first. But once you start, it becomes monumentally freeing, because it begins to give you a bird's-eye view from which you can plan your ministry year, which in turn liberates you from the tyranny of the urgent. Imagine—freedom from both the tyranny of the new and the tyranny of the urgent!

Recommended Reading for Section 2

ON WORSHIP

Carson, D. A. *Worship: Adoration and Action* (Eugene, OR: Wipf & Stock, 2002).

Carson, D. A., ed. *Worship by the Book* (Grand Rapids, MI: Zondervan, 2002).

Croft, Brian, and Jason Adkins. *Gather God's People: Understand, Plan, and Lead Worship in Your Local Church* (Grand Rapids, MI: Zondervan, 2015).

Davies, Horton. *The Worship of the American Puritans* (Morgan, PA: Soli Deo Gloria, 2003).

Davies, Horton. *The Worship of the English Puritans* (Morgan, PA: Soli Deo Gloria, 2003).

Gibson, Jonathan, and Mark Earngey, eds. *Reformation Worship: Liturgies from the Past for the Present* (Greensboro, NC: New Growth Press, 2018).

Merker, Matt. *Corporate Worship: The Church Gathers as God's People* (Wheaton, IL: Crossway, 2021).

Peterson, David. *Engaging with God: A Biblical Theology of Worship* (Downers Grove, IL: InterVarsity Press, 1992).

Ryken, Philip Graham, Derek W. H. Thomas, and J. Ligon Duncan III, eds. *Give Praise to God: A Vision for Reforming Worship* (Phillipsburg, NJ: Presbyterian & Reformed, 2003).

ON MUSIC

Janssen, Brian V. *Sing a New (Covenant) Song: Thinking About the Songs We Sing to God* (Hospers, IA: Self-published, 2002). To obtain copies, contact the author at janssenb@nethtc.net.

Master's Seminary, *Hymns of Grace* (Los Angeles: Master's Seminary Press, 2015).

Sovereign Grace Ministries Music (www.sovereigngraceministries.org/music/).

Trinity Hymnal (Suwanee, GA: Great Commission Publications, 1990).

ON PASTORING

Bridges, Charles. *The Christian Ministry* (Carlisle, PA: Banner of Truth, 2001).

Spurgeon, C. H. *An All-Round Ministry* (Carlisle, PA: Banner of Truth, 1981).

Spurgeon, C. H. *Lectures to My Students* (Grand Rapids, MI: Zondervan, 1979).

SECTION 3

GATHERING ELDERS

14

The Importance of Elders

IT IS POPULAR IN SOME contemporary circles to hold that church leadership structures really just boil down to semantics. Whether you call them deacons or elders is largely immaterial, as long as you have some spiritually mature people leading the church and conducting its affairs. In Baptist circles, and particularly in Southern Baptist churches over the last 120 years, the prevalent leadership model seems to be a single pastor/elder supported by multiple deacons and often held accountable by a board of trustees.

Granted, the Bible leaves ample room to wiggle on the issue of church structure. But although the evidence is scant, it is nevertheless consistent. New Testament churches are to be congregationally governed yet led by a plurality of elders who are released by servant deacons to devote themselves to the ministry of the Word and prayer.[1]

In this section, we begin to think about the need for gathering a plurality of elders and how to go about gathering them with biblical wisdom. In this chapter, we'll focus particularly on reviewing the biblical data and reflecting on the practical benefits of having a plurality of nonstaff elders.

Brief Biblical Background

Acts 20:17–38 shows that the words translated as "elders" (*presbuterous*, v. 17) and "overseers" (*episkopous*, v. 28 [also known as bishops]) are interchangeable, and that both do the work of pastoring (*poimainein*, v. 28) or shepherding God's flock. A pastor, then, is an elder, and an elder is a bishop/overseer—all three terms refer to the same office and the same work of pastoring.[2] Note, too, that Paul "sent to Ephesus" for "the elders [*presbuterous*, plural] of the church [*ekklēsias*, singular]" (v. 17). The pattern is of a plurality of elders in each local church.[3]

First Timothy 3:1–13 distinguishes the office of elder (*episkopos*) from that of deacon (*diakonos*). Each must meet the same character requirements, but elders must also be able to teach[4]—an ability not required for the office of deacon. In fact, D. A. Carson has observed that all the qualities Paul lays out for elders are elsewhere in the New Testament enjoined on all Christians—every quality, that is, except the ability to teach. Right away, then, we see that elders are different from deacons in that teaching is pivotal to the elder's responsibility, while the deacon's tasks lie elsewhere. Both offices must be present for a church to be organized, led, and served according to the Word.

Acts 6:1–4 further clarifies the distinction. There we read of a controversy between Greek and Hebrew widows about the equity of food distribution among them. The disciples gather the whole congregation and say, "It is not desirable for us to neglect the word of God in order to serve [*diakonein*] tables. Therefore, brethren, select from among you seven men of good reputation, full of the Spirit and of wisdom, whom we may put in charge of this task. But we will devote ourselves to prayer and to the ministry [*diakonia*] of the word" (6:2–4). The division of labor is clear. The seven chosen men "deaconed" (served) tables, which released the apostles for "deaconing" the Word.

Deacons, then, serve to care for the physical and financial needs of the church, and they do so in a way that heals divisions, brings unity under the Word, and supports the leadership of the elders. Without this practical service of the deacons, the elders will not be freed to devote themselves to praying and serving the Word to people. Elders need deacons to serve practically, and deacons need elders to lead spiritually.

Think Tank

1. Read Acts 14:23. What does this imply about the way Paul structured the churches he planted?

2. Look up at least five of the following verses: Acts 11:30; 16:4; 20:17; 21:18; Philippians 1:1; Titus 1:5; James 5:14; 1 Peter 5:1. What do you learn about the number and responsibilities of elders in local churches?

3. Compare Acts 20:17 and 28. Then compare Titus 1:5, 6, and 7. What terms seem to be used interchangeably?

The Practicality of Plurality

We've seen some of the main biblical arguments for the distinction between elders and deacons, for the roles of each, and for a plurality of elders in a single church.[5] What are the practical benefits of having more than one elder in each church? In other words, is it worth the trouble to switch from a single-pastor/multiple-deacon leadership structure to a plurality of elders leadership structure with multiple serving deacons?[6] Let's think about some of the advantages of making the switch.

It balances pastoral weakness. No pastor is broadly gifted enough to do all the work of the ministry equally well by himself. There are weaknesses in every pastor's game. We all need other people to balance out our all-too-human deficiencies. When you surround yourself with godly men whose gifts, passions, and abilities balance yours, you provide more well-rounded leadership for people to follow.

It diffuses congregational criticism. Under the single-pastor/multiple-deacon model, the pastor often takes the brunt of the criticism alone. Tough decisions can be misperceived, motives can be misconstrued, and before too long the pastor becomes the target of all the critical remarks because he is the one who is perceived to be making all the decisions and casting all the final votes—and under this model, he often is. Within a plurality of elders, however, leadership is shared with a body of nonstaff elders who have been recognized and affirmed by the congregation. This provision alleviates the pastor from bearing all the criticism, because now leadership and decision-making responsibility are shared among the group. Other men can now stand in the gap with the pastor, and they can take both responsibility and criticism together. Also, the congregation likely will be more willing to follow the tough decisions of a group of both staff and nonstaff elders than to follow those made alone by a paid pastor. So some criticism may be avoided simply by the increased trust that a plurality of congregationally recognized nonstaff elders engenders among church members.

It adds pastoral wisdom. Sharing leadership with a group of godly, able nonstaff elders will almost invariably keep pastors (especially young ones) from saying or doing dumb things, or from saying or doing the right things in unhelpful ways. None of us is omniscient. We all need to humble ourselves, share leadership, and ask advice. In fact, many of us are impatient when it comes to implementing a vision for godly change. Godly elders can help us select a pace for change that the congregation can keep up with. They can also help us formulate plans, articulate goals, and handle sensitive situations better than we may do if left to ourselves.

It indigenizes leadership. That is, it roots leadership in nonstaff members. This is important because the congregation needs to be able to function and continue to grow even if something awful happens to the paid pastor. The last thing we want to do as vocational pastors is to make the congregation so dependent on us that the church would fall apart if we died, got called somewhere else, or (God forbid) fell into some disqualifying sin. We want our work to continue to bear fruit long after we're gone! But that means leadership must be rooted in nonstaff members. The best, most biblical way to do that is to incorporate a structure of leadership based on a plurality of elders in which the nonstaff elders outnumber the staff elders.

It enables corrective discipline. Without corrective discipline, the church has no way to protect the purity of her public corporate witness from the hypocrisy of members involved in scandalous sin. Yet the discharge of corrective church discipline is far more difficult without a plurality of elders. Performing corrective church discipline requires a leadership structure that won't buckle under the spiritual and relational pressures of the process. By adding wisdom, diffusing criticism, balancing pastoral weaknesses, and indigenizing leadership, plural eldership helps transfer the load of corrective discipline across multiple pillars. Plural eldership, then, is critical for the discharge of corrective discipline and therefore is critical for maintaining the corporate witness of the local church in the eyes of the unbelieving community as well.

It defuses "us vs. him." When disagreements happen between a pastor and the congregation regarding the direction of the church or a difficult decision that affects the whole congregation, an unhealthy "us vs. him" mentality can crop up. This can make the pastor feel extremely isolated and can often breed adversarial attitudes underneath a surface of congenial pastor/congregation relationships. Granted, a plurality of elders may simply shift the relationship into the "us vs. *them*" gear. However, it relieves the isolation of the pastor, and it may prevent such antipathies from ever arising if the pastor is wise enough to receive godly counsel. Again, by adding wisdom, diffusing criticism, balancing pastoral weaknesses, and indigenizing leadership, a plurality of elders can go a long way toward defusing the "us vs. him" bomb.

Think Tank

1. How could you envision a plurality of elders being healthy for your church corporately?

2. How could you envision a plurality of elders being healthy for you as a pastor?

3. What are some obstacles that are keeping you from moving toward a plurality of elders?

4. What are some ways that you can start praying for healthy change in your church?

Conclusion

Churches can get away with not having elders. It happens all the time. But the biblical pattern is consistent and the practical benefits are clear, both for the pastor and for the congregation. The question, then, isn't why should we have elders, but why *shouldn't* we? I can honestly say that moving to a plurality of elders in our church has been the single most helpful event to me in my pastoral ministry here in Washington, DC.

When the idea of plural eldership is proposed, some pastors respond by pointing out the difficulty of transitioning from other models to an elder-led model. How do you go about choosing elders? Is there a viable process for agreeing on who should serve? We turn to these questions and several more in our next four chapters.

15

Looking for a Few Good Men

IT SEEMS PASTORS TODAY are looking in almost every direction for help on how to instill a vision, draw a crowd, lead a church, and change a culture. In the process, they often find competing ideas of both what it takes and what it means to be a leader in the church. As we saw in the previous chapter, eldership is the biblical model for church leadership. The question we want to ask in this chapter is, how do you go about looking for elders, and what exactly is it that you're looking for?

Recognizing before Training

Every pastor is responsible for developing nonstaff leadership in the church.[1] It can sometimes seem intuitive for pastors to take a training attitude toward developing elders in particular. That is, choose a candidate based perhaps on faithfulness in attendance, availability for service, and teachability, guide him through a one- or two-year training program, and then nominate and confirm him as an elder to learn the rest of the material on the job.

Of course, there's nothing inherently wrong with this strategy. In fact, discipling people is something we should be doing, and training the elders that we've recognized is an integral part of pastoral responsibility (2 Tim. 2:2). But it may be wise to *recognize* men who are already qualified and are already doing elder-type work rather than to "make" men elders simply by training them. In other words, you are looking not just for untapped potential, but for a positive reason a man should be an elder.

Paul says, "The sins of some men are quite evident, going before them to judgment; for others, their sins follow after. Likewise also, deeds that are good are quite evident, and those which are otherwise cannot be concealed" (1 Tim. 5:24–25). These words come in the context of appointing elders. Paul is teaching Timothy to recognize elder-quality men—as well as those who don't qualify—by their behavior.

By *recognizing* elders before we train them, we're simply acknowledging that a man is already living with elder-quality character and doing elder-type relational work without having the title. By *training* elders before we recognize them as such, we're taking a man who may not have displayed any of these character traits or discipling habits and trying to mold him into a shape he hasn't yet taken. Gathering elders by recognition enables us to spot those men in the congregation who are already proving by their lifestyle that they are elders in deed, even if not in title. Their actions give evidence that God is raising them up for leadership in the church, and their selfless concern for the church's corporate life tips us off that they have an elder's outlook and maturity.

These are the best kind of men to have as elders, because they view eldering not simply as an office to train for and execute, but also as a wise and godly way to live regardless of their official capacity. This is the kind of man who is most likely to be fruitful and faithful as an official elder. He has adopted an eldering lifestyle before ever assuming the office and so is likely to continue in that lifestyle long after his official tenure has ended.

Immediately, though, the question is raised: What if there aren't any of this kind of men to be recognized in our local church? What other option do I have but to train? The best course to pursue in this case is to keep preaching the Word faithfully, keep engaging in personal discipleship and teaching men what it means to be mature in the Lord, keep praying that the Lord would raise up men like this, and keep looking for them. Perhaps examine your own standards for eldership—are your standards higher than the Bible requires them to be? Keep preaching. Keep praying. Keep developing a culture of personal discipleship, and keep being patient.

So what are we supposed to be recognizing? What exactly is an elder? We might be wise to start by dispelling a few common myths.

What Is an Elder *Not*?

A biblical elder is not simply an older male. There are plenty of godly older men who do meet the character qualifications for biblical eldership. I hope the Lord blesses our church with more! But bare chronological advancement, even when married to upstanding church membership, is not sufficient to satisfy the requirements outlined in 1 Timothy 3 and Titus 1. In fact, there are some thirty-year-old men (or even younger) who are more qualified to be elders than some men twice their age. Life experience alone does not qualify a man to be an elder.

A biblical elder is not simply a successful businessman. In fact, some of the very principles or character traits that get some businessmen to the top of the business ladder may actually put them on the bottom rung of the church leadership ladder.[2] We're not looking for people who "know what they want and know how to get it." Nor are we looking for people who know how to manage people, raise money, climb the ladder, or close the deal. Leadership in the church is fundamentally different than leadership in the business world (Mark 10:35–45; John 13:1–17). The church is not simply a nonprofit business. It is the body of Christ, and as such it is the most unique corporate institution in the world. It operates on principles of distinctively Christian doctrine, servanthood, holiness, faith, hope, and love. This is not, of course, to say that it is impossible to be a biblically qualified elder and a successful businessman at the same time. It is simply to say that success and leadership in the business world do not always or necessarily guarantee success in eldership in the local church.

A biblical elder is not simply an involved community member. Being elected to sit on a city or neighborhood council is a wonderful privilege and a unique evangelistic opportunity for any Christian. But again, such an achievement is neither necessary nor sufficient for meeting the qualifications of elder. A man can be the president of the PTA, coach Little League baseball, be an alderman, and lead a Boy Scout troop and still not be qualified as an elder. Serving the community in these ways certainly doesn't preclude a man from qualifying. But as we look around to see who might meet the biblical requirements, community service alone cannot be our ultimate criterion.

A biblical elder is not simply a "good ol' boy." Living in the same location and having the same friends or even being a member of the same church for thirty-plus years doesn't make a man an elder. Serving in the capacity of elder in a local church should not be dependent on whether a man is willing to "play ball," is a part of the right social network, or is from the right part of the country (or county, depending on where you live!). Likeability can often be deceptive.

A biblical elder is not a female. The criteria laid out in 1 Timothy 3:1–7 and Titus 1:6–9 assume male leadership in the church. The office of elder requires the ones holding it to be able to teach. Teaching is an authoritative act, and women are forbidden to exercise authority over men in the church (1 Tim. 2:9–15). Paul roots that prohibition in the order of creation in Genesis 1 and 2: Adam was created before Eve, revealing Adam's God-given place of headship over her. Both are equally created in the image of God, but God has given them different yet complementary roles to fill both in the home and in the church.[3]

A biblical elder is not a politician. The biblical office of elder is an elected office. But the man who fills it should not be one who subtly or overtly campaigns for it, or one who is noticeably vocal about promoting political positions in the context of the local church.

Think Tank

1. How does your church choose its leaders? What are the dominant criteria? Why these?

2. What must a man believe in order to be an elder in your church?

What *Is* an Elder?

What, then, is a biblical elder? That question can be answered first in terms of the office and second in terms of the man. The office of elder is designed for the leadership of the church through the teaching of the Word.[4] The character of the man who qualifies to fulfill that office is described in 1 Timothy 3:1–7 and Titus 1:6–9. An elder is simply a man of exemplary, Christlike character who is able to lead God's people by teaching them God's Word in a way that profits them spiritually. So we are looking for men who *display* exemplary character and who *demonstrate* both aptitude and fruitfulness in teaching God's Word.[5] This definition might serve as a good spiritual snapshot or profile of the kind of men you're looking for to be elders.

Qualification Quadrants

A helpful way to think about the criteria for choosing leaders might be in terms of the quadrants in Figure 15.1. Again, the call to being an elder is a call to leadership through biblical teaching. This means that, at a bare minimum, you need men who, first and foremost, share a deep, biblical understanding of the fundamentals of Christian theology and the gospel. Areas to consider first are the authority and sufficiency of Scripture, God's sovereignty, the divinity and exclusivity of Christ, and the atonement. No man who falters in the basics of biblical doctrine should be considered for eldership, no matter how gifted or likeable he may be. The Word builds the church, and as such, it simply can't be healthy for any of our elders to have reservations about fundamental Christian truths.

Once it has been determined that a candidate is sound in the central Bible doctrines, it is our practice to confirm that the candidate shares our particular doctrinal distinctives—in our case, for instance, the necessity of believers' baptism for local church membership. These issues, while not necessary for salvation, are nevertheless important for how we decide to conduct our life together as a church. Such distinctives will obviously vary depending on the convictions of the congregation. The principle, however, is simply that the leaders of a congregation should understand and be conscientious advocates of a local church's distinctive doctrines. The elders need to agree on these matters so that their own unity doesn't fracture, and so that they can provide a unified lead for the congregation to follow.

Core Theology	**Doctrinal Distinctives**
• Authority and Sufficiency of Scripture	• Believers' Baptism
• God's Sovereignty	• Congregationalism
• Divinity and Exclusivity of Christ	
• The Atonement	
Love for the Congregation	**Cultural Distinctives**
• Attending Regularly	• Gender Roles in the Home and Church
• Discipling Selflessly	• Opposition to Homosexuality
• Serving Consistently	

Figure 15.1—Qualification Quadrants

Third, it is extremely helpful to ensure that the candidate is courageous enough to stand against the culture on certain clear biblical issues, such as the role of women in the church. An elder must model for the congregation both a strength and a willingness to live a countercultural lifestyle in areas where Christ and culture conflict. If, as an elder, a man caves in to the conforming pressures of the culture on well-defined biblical issues, his example and teaching will eventually lead the church to look more like the world.

Finally, we need to be able to discern from the candidate's relational involvement in the church that he loves the congregation. We want to be able to recognize his love for the other members of the church by the fact that he's already involved in doing elder-type work even before he's given the title. So we might reasonably expect a man who is recognized as an elder to be attending regularly, initiating with others to do them spiritual good, and serving the church as faithfully as he can.

Think Tank

1. What's the difference between recognizing elders and training them?

2. Why might it be wise to recognize rather than train elders?

3. Who in your church might be qualified to serve as an elder?

Conclusion

One of the most significant human dynamics in the church's continuing spiritual growth and health is the kind of leadership it is following. When biblically qualified men are leading a church with character and skill, it is a deep and wide blessing for the unity, holiness, and spiritual growth of the church. Put somewhat negatively, *so many* potential mistakes and heartaches can be avoided simply by ensuring that only those men who are biblically qualified become elders.

Choosing elders, then, is a pivotal time in the life of a developing church—so much so, in fact, that we will continue to think about assessing the character, ability, and fit of potential elders in the pages that follow.

16

Assessment

CHURCHES RARELY GROW PAST the maturity of their leaders. It may be possible, but it certainly is not likely. The implication is that choosing elders can be either a significant help or a significant hindrance to the maturity and growth of the congregation. Mature, able leaders will model godly behavior and teach sound doctrine, which will promote congregational health and growth. Conversely, immature leaders who are less than able to teach will model behavior that may not be above reproach and will teach doctrine that may not conform to godliness, both of which will likely put a low cap on the maturity level of the members, because they're not hearing sound doctrine or seeing it lived out by their leaders.

Pastors, then, need to realize that elder selection is critical for the corporate health of the church. The process *must* be governed by biblical criteria and carried out in a wise, patient, and winsome manner. In this chapter, we'll look briefly at assessing the character, ability, and fit of a potential elder. Chapter 17 will further address why character is particularly crucial, and chapter 18 will walk us through the process of installing new elders.

Assessing Character

A good candidate for the office of elder is known by his behavior (1 Tim. 5:24–25), because his behavior reveals his character, and character is largely what makes an elder. Reputation with outsiders is important (3:7). But this requirement should not justify nominating a man simply because he's an honest business leader in the community. He may indeed be an established business leader, but is he argumentative? Is he given to excess in any way? Is he hospitable with his home and his financial resources? Is he gentle in both speech and conduct? Does he love money by chasing after it, keeping exorbitant amounts of it to himself, or spending lavishly on himself? Is he self-controlled? Is he kind to all? Is he patient when he's wronged? All these questions are direct implications of the character criteria found in 1 Timothy 3:1–7 and 2 Timothy 2:24–25.

Think Tank

1. Read 1 Timothy 3:1–7. Why is it particularly important for elders to be gentle and not quarrelsome?

2. Read 2 Timothy 2:24–25. Why is it important for elders not to be resentful?

We might dig around elsewhere in the Bible for wisdom in discerning lifestyle habits that evidence an elder's heart. Does the man evidence a love for God and for the church by faithfully attending church meetings as a committed member (Heb. 10:24–25; John 13:34–35; 1 John 4:20–21)? Does he contribute to the corporate spiritual health of the church by the way he treats and speaks with others (Phil. 2:1–5; Eph. 4:29)? Does he use his words to build up by pointing out evidences of God's grace in others, or to tear down by constant criticism? Is he meeting together with younger or struggling Christians to do them good spiritually (Ezek. 34)? Does he watch out for the spiritual lives of other people (Acts 20:28)? Does he pray for the church and its members regularly? Is he able to share the gospel clearly with unbelievers, and does he do that regularly? Is he growing in his knowledge of God and fruitfulness in personal ministry in the church (Col. 1:9–14)? Is he an influence for division or for unity? Does he exercise godly wisdom that is "first pure, then peaceable, gentle, reasonable, full of mercy and good fruits, unwavering, without hypocrisy" (James 3:17)? Does the man show the humility of wisdom by being easy to correct, or is he pridefully recalcitrant in his own opinions (Prov. 12:1)? In short, is this man setting an example for other church members "in speech, conduct, love, faith and purity" (1 Tim. 4:12; cf. 1 Pet. 5:1–5)?[1] If not, it's best to be patient and keep looking.

This carefulness is an effort to obey Paul's injunction to Timothy: "Do not lay hands upon anyone too hastily and thereby share responsibility for the sins of others; keep yourself free from sin" (1 Tim. 5:22). It is better to be patient in waiting for God to raise up other elders than to share in the guilt of mistakes in shepherding made by prematurely appointed men (cf. Heb. 13:17).

Assessing Ability

As we assess character, we also need to be assessing a man's ability to teach. There is, of course, a sense in which we must already have a level of assurance about a man's character before ever putting him up front to teach. So he needs to be attending faithfully as a member, evidently concerned about and involved in the corporate life of the church, not known for any particularly public or scandalous character flaw, and doctrinally sound. He needs to be a man we know to be faithful in private Bible reading and prayer, to be maintaining a faithful and obedient evangelical witness at work, and to be living a holy lifestyle.

Once we've gathered this basic character information, we can feel reasonably confident about giving a man, whether young or old, opportunity to try out his teaching gifts, and an opportunity for us to test them. This testing is in accordance with 1 Timothy 3:10: "They [deacons] must first be tested; and then if there is nothing against them, let them serve as deacons" (NIV 1984). If deacons must be tested as servants in the physical and financial matters of the church, then it seems a good and necessary implication that potential elders must be tested regarding their fitness and ability to minister the Word.

What then does it mean to be "able to teach" (1 Tim. 3:2)? Many have thought that such teaching must necessarily mean formal, public, expositional preaching. While this may be included, it is not the necessary or exclusive definition of "able to teach." Ability to teach the Word simply means that a man is able to explain the Scriptures accurately to other people in ways that profit them spiritually. He should be known by others in the congregation as a man to whom people can go in order to have the Scriptures explained to them. This could mean that a man is gifted to preach. But it may also mean that a man has an effective and broad-based discipling ministry within the church, in which he is explaining and applying the Scriptures to individuals in ways that help them grow in Christian knowledge, love, and fruitfulness. It may mean he is fruitful as a curriculum writer or small-group leader or discipler.

With this understanding of what it means to be able to teach, we can see how some elders simply end up in *public* teaching situations more often than others. Yet for the development of their authority among the congregation, it is wise to choose men who are at least willing to teach publicly and who show some modicum of interest and propensity to do so. Again, all authority in the church belongs to Jesus Christ, and he mediates that authority to his undershepherds through his Word. Since the authority of the elder is derived from his handling of the Scriptures, he does need to be able to teach publicly, even if infrequently, simply in order that his authority might be shown to derive from the Word of God and his accurate handling of it (not from the strength of his personality or the success of his business ventures).

Adult education times and Sunday evening services are normally the best contexts in which to test a man's public teaching gifts. Small-group leadership, or apprenticeship with a small-group leader, can also be helpful and effective ways of discerning whether or not a man is able to teach. But giving him such opportunities will not prove optimally fruitful unless a qualified man is in the class or service to observe him teaching and is available afterward to give him constructive feedback on which to build for further growth in aptitude.[2]

We are also wise to observe how frequently and effectively a man uses hospitality to do other members or visitors spiritual good (1 Tim. 3:2), and how involved he is in discipling younger men, providing accountability for them, and modeling godly behavior for them. We should feel free to ask both the candidate and others in the congregation about these matters.[3] Asking members for their input shows humility in the way you lead and may enable you to make a wiser, more informed decision on whom to recommend to the congregation as potential elders.

Assessing Fit

Having examined a candidate's character and ability, it is then time to assess whether or not the man would fit well in the context of the current elders. Two important considerations predominate here—gifting/passion and communication style, both relative to the other elders.

Regarding gifts and passions, it is always helpful to have a balance represented among the eldership. Among our elders, one is unusually gifted and motivated for missions work, one has pronounced administrative talents, one is more meticulous in theological and procedural accuracy, one is a big-picture visionary with plans for discipleship and preaching, others bring pronounced decision-making skills, and so on. The point is that the nonstaff elders are balancing the weaknesses of the main teaching pastor, and the weaknesses among the elders are hopefully not shared by all. If all are unusually gifted for the same thing, then other important considerations will almost invariably be neglected in the routine decision-making process.

Regarding communication style, it will be wise to note how a potential elder interacts with the rest of the group. Is he confident and insistent or reluctant and understated? Does he tend to take it all in and then give his opinion or does he tend to be one of the first to share his ideas? Does he facilitate consensus by synthesizing the common thoughts and opinions of others or does he point out important distinctions? Is he a submissive follower, an independent thinker, a balancing contrarian, or a polarizing contrarian? The list could go on.

Of course, in order to observe his gifts and communication patterns relative to the other elders, you'll have to see him actually interacting with them. To that end, it may be wise to invite potential elders to actually participate in one or two elders' meetings as a sort of trial run to observe how their presence might contribute to the dynamic of the conversation. Is it elucidating, helpful, unifying, edifying, and productive? Or might it be distracting, too forceful, unhelpfully quiet, obscuring, and generally not as useful as you had hoped?

In our church, we've made it an informal requirement to have unanimity among the elders in order to move ahead with nominating a new elder for congregational affirmation. This requirement is merely a prudential one—we've not written it into our constitution. But let's say a current elder, Tom, thinks a potential new elder, Bill, is not qualified for the office. Bill gets nominated anyway, and the congregation affirms him. Tom may be able to work well with Bill, even though Tom thinks Bill is underqualified. But Tom's disagreement with the decision to nominate Bill introduces the potential for unnecessary friction among the group that can lead to the fracturing of unity among the elders, and potentially among the congregation.

Conclusion

Hopefully we've helped establish that the process of assessing candidates for eldership should be driven primarily by biblical qualifications. No matter how well a potential candidate may "fit" into the current eldership, that fit will prove false if he is not qualified in both character and ability. Building a healthy church is in large part a matter of putting into place a biblical leadership structure and filling it with biblically qualified people. This is not simply being pragmatic; rather, it is being deliberately biblical about how we organize ourselves, what we understand to be the prerequisites for Christian leadership, and consequently whom we look to as leaders.

When it comes to assessing potential elders, this deliberateness takes the form of asking specific biblical questions about a man's character and ability, not simply questions about personality, reputation in the business world, political savvy, or the like. Being a deliberate church means being careful about allowing the Word of God to drive both our search for and our assessment of men who would serve as potential elders.

17

Why Character Is Crucial

IT WOULD BE EASY TO BEAT potential elder candidates—or even ourselves!—over the head with the club of 1 Timothy 3:1–7. If we take these requirements to their extremes, then obviously no one would ever qualify to be an elder, because no one meets them perfectly in thought, word, attitude, and action. So a word of caution about unrealistic standards is appropriate.

Having said that, we agree with D. A. Carson, who is fond of observing that perhaps the most extraordinary thing about the biblical prerequisites for elders is that they are not all that extraordinary. Certainly it isn't too much to ask a man to be self-controlled, not addicted to alcohol or money, able to control his temper, gentle, faithful to his wife or chaste in his singleness, patient, and the like.

Moreover, the work of the elder actually demands the exercise of these character qualities. In this chapter, we stop to think about what exactly it is about being an elder that requires both character and behavior that is "above reproach" (1 Tim. 3:2).

Modeling

The primary practical reason that character is so important in an elder is that modeling godliness for others is central to his work.

He is to "set an *example* for the believers in speech, in life, in love, in faith, and in purity" (1 Tim. 4:12 NIV 1984). He is to shepherd God's flock in a way that is "eager to serve; not lording it over those entrusted to [him], but being [an *example*] to the flock" (1 Pet. 5:2–3 NIV 1984; cf. Titus 2:7–8). Paul wrote to the Thessalonians, "you know how we lived among you *for your sake*." And his deliberate example had its intended effect, because they became "*imitators* of us and of the Lord" (1 Thess. 1:5–6 NIV 1984). Elders lead first and foremost by example.

The examples set by the elders will be significant in helping shape the congregation's idea of what spiritual maturity looks like. An elder may set a good example or a bad example, but he will not be able to avoid setting one or the other. As elders model holiness in lifestyle, gentleness in speech, selflessness in relationships, soundness in doctrine, and a loving concern for other members of the congregation, the church will be encouraged to think of godliness in like manner, and the pastor's preaching will be illustrated by these moving pictures of godliness. Conversely, if an elder models questionable lifestyle choices, quarrelsome speech, and preoccupation with getting his own needs met, the church will be instructed to think of godliness in this way, and the pastor's preaching will likely be contradicted by the false image of maturity projected by such an elder.

The examples set by elders will also be significant in developing the corporate witness of the church in the surrounding community. As church members follow the examples of their leaders, their behavior will usually become either more or less godly, depending on the examples being set. The examples of the elders will begin to cultivate a corporate culture among the congregation that is watered at least in part by their own character, speech, and behavior as leaders. Over time, that corporate culture will become more and more evident to the surrounding community as members interact with their neighbors and model Christianity for them.

What will your church be known for in the community ten years from now? Will it be distinctively Christian love, holiness, and doctrine? Or will your church simply be a reflection of the culture? The answer, in large part, lies in the character modeled by the elders. Are they modeling distinctively Christian love, holiness, and doctrine? Or are they simply reflections of the culture?

Think Tank

1. Read Ezekiel 34:1–10. What were Israel's shepherds failing to do?

2. What implications does this passage have for pastoral ministry today?

Meetings

Let's face it: elders' meetings can be pretty dicey affairs. Making group decisions about budget percentages, discipline cases, and the direction of the church can test the patience and gentleness of even the best of men. This is one of the reasons that you want to make sure only men of godly character, as defined by 1 Timothy 3:1–7 and Titus 1:6–9, are privy to the conversation.

The criterion of not being quarrelsome is particularly important here (1 Tim. 3:3; 2 Tim. 2:24). In our circles, normally sized elder bodies consist of anywhere between three and twelve men. We know they can get much larger in other churches (particularly in churches that distinguish between teaching and ruling elders). When you get even five or six men together to discuss issues of member care and to strategize for the spread of the gospel, stating opinions and beliefs in mature ways becomes of towering importance. Many elder bodies have experienced unnecessary division simply because some of the men who have been appointed to the office are not yet able to state beliefs or opinions without becoming quarrelsome or fractious. Gentle spirits who are deliberate in choosing their words, their tone, and their perspective, even if not the most learned or articulate of the group, are much to be preferred over those who may be both learned and articulate but are argumentative.

Temperateness (1 Tim. 3:2) is also of marked significance during elders' meetings. Every elder needs to be able to discuss emotionally and theologically loaded situations with a cool temper and a level head. Paul encourages Timothy to "keep your head in all situations" (2 Tim. 4:5 NIV 1984). This is part of the demeanor to which every elder is called. Short tempers and unbridled tongues are virtual omens of strife. But a man who is slow to anger, just like his Lord, will be of inestimable value when the screws of sin seek to tighten their grip in the heat of intense conversations.

None of this, of course, is to say that a particularly intense person is necessarily precluded from being an elder simply by virtue of his personality. Some of our elders are overtly competitive, intensely opinionated, and emotionally animated. Yet they are all able to control both their tempers and their tongues during potentially volatile discussions.

Elders meet together regularly. Be careful, then, to choose men with the character to handle conversations in which unqualified men might sully their testimony or create discord by their own demeanor.

The Great Meeting

The most compelling reason of all that character is crucial for elders is our accountability to God. Elders are men who must "give an account" to God for the way they exercise oversight of his flock (Heb. 13:17). If the undershepherds set a pace that's too fast for the sheep; if they treat the sheep harshly and without compassion or grace; or if they are unfaithful in executing their responsibilities or unholy in the way they model the Christian life, then the Great Shepherd will see it—and he will hold them accountable (Jer. 23:1–4).

As teachers, elders "will incur a stricter judgment" (James 3:1), which implies that God will, in some sense, hold teachers to a higher standard of holiness. If a man has great public teaching gifts and yet is known to be characteristically argumentative, impure in speech, or unable to control his appetites, then it would be unwise to nominate him for eldership. Immature teachers make the most notable hypocrites. And if we allow those who are immature to teach and model a doctrine that does not conform to godliness, then we share the guilt of their failure to feed God's sheep in green pastures, which will bring on us his intense, fatherly displeasure (1 Tim. 5:22; Jer. 23:9–40; Ezek. 34).

Paul was acutely aware of the coming day when he would finally be assessed by his great Master. In fact, it is to this coming day of judgment that he appeals to quell the controversy in Corinth over who was baptized by whom. He says,

> But to me it is a very small thing that I may be examined by you, or by any human court; in fact, I do not even examine myself. For I am conscious of nothing against myself, yet I am not by this acquitted; but the one who examines me is the Lord. Therefore do not go on passing judgment before the time, but wait until the Lord comes who will both bring to light the things hidden in the darkness and disclose the motives of men's hearts; and then each man's praise will come to him from God. (1 Cor. 4:3–5; cf. 2 Cor. 5:9–10)

In the context of instructing the Corinthians to abandon their partisan spirit, Paul reveals his awareness of his own accountability to God, which released him from slavery to the thoughts and opinions of man (i.e., the fear of man) and motivated him to prove himself faithful as a godly leader. Considering his accountability to God enabled Paul to respond to criticism and human judgment with godly patience rather than bitterness or anger.

Think Tank

1. Read Jeremiah 23. What were the shepherds and prophets supposed to be doing?

2. How had they failed to obey God in the responsibility he had given them?

3. What aspect of his character does God emphasize to his servants in verses 23–24 as a result?

4. What are some implications of Jeremiah 23 for pastors today?

Every elder needs to realize that his ministry will be finally evaluated not by what other people think or how they respond, but by God himself. On that day, God will "bring to light the things hidden in the darkness and disclose the motives of men's hearts" (1 Cor. 4:5). All an elder's attitudes, motives, desires, inclinations, and decisions—every idle word that he speaks under his breath or even thinks in his mind—will be disclosed, and he will be laid bare for examination by his God and Master. Anticipating the reality of God's evaluation both of the elder and of his ministry is the ultimate motivation for a life characterized by meticulous godliness.

Conclusion

Praise God for Christ's righteousness credited to our account! Without it, no one would ever qualify to be an elder in God's church. Still, part of being a deliberate church means being carefully biblical about who becomes an elder and why. No church is perfect, and you may very well make a mistake (or multiple mistakes!) in the process of determining who is qualified to lead as an elder. But elders who display godly character are a tremendous blessing to the church, primarily because they live exemplary Christian lives that other members can imitate as they follow Christ.

Not only do godly elders provide an example—they also prevent much division and strife by handling potentially volatile situations with care. Their humility makes them difficult to offend; their holiness makes them easy to trust; their gentle speech makes them easy to hear as sources of correction or critique; and their hospitality provides a context for spiritual encouragement and edification. Being deliberate about the godliness of our leaders matters not only because it builds up the church but also because it *liberates* her from the tyranny of selfish ambition and vain conceit—which in turn frees her from the contentious divisions that originate from the unchecked desires and motives of biblically unqualified men (Phil. 2:1–5; James 4:1–3). And over time, godly elders will lead the church by their own Christlike example into an ever-increasing freedom from the sin that so easily entangles, until we are forever released from our corruption by the return of the King, who will take us up to be perfected in the city whose architect and builder is God.

18

Getting Started

HAVING ESTABLISHED SOMETHING of the importance and character of elders, as well as a method of looking for them, how then do you transition out of a less faithful model of church leadership into an elder-led model? In this chapter, we will discuss five broad stages of pastoral leadership that are helpful to remember in making the jump.[1]

It will be wise for us, as well, to remember that this process may need to take a considerable amount of time. Many congregations have never known any other structure of leadership besides a single pastor, a board of deacons, and a board of trustees. So if you are a new pastor of an old congregation, step gingerly here. Adjust your own expectations so that you are ready for the process to take five years or, in particularly difficult cases, more. Growth takes time. Take a long-term perspective. Commit yourself to the people and to the process, and love them well by providing them with particularly patient instruction in these matters.

Exposition

You cannot expect anyone in an evangelical church to follow you into change until you've taught them from the Bible why that change is necessary and good.[2] Particularly when you are entering a well-established church that has developed cherished but unbiblical traditions, the members need to be convinced that you are leading them into a way of doing things that is more biblically faithful, not less so. In fact, biblical teaching is quite often the only way that members will give up cherished but unbiblical patterns of leadership and organization.

This doesn't mean that your first sermon as the new pastor should be on 1 Timothy 3:1–7. It means that you prove yourself first to be a faithful preacher of the gospel, calling boldly for repentance and belief, taking the point of the selected text as the point of each of your sermons, and preaching those sermons in a way that naturally leads to a clear presentation of the gospel as an implication of the text. If some members of the church are not Christians, this will give them an opportunity to either be converted by the gospel or leave because they're offended by it. If other members of the church are Christians, then preaching the point of the text as the point of the sermon with evangelistic punch will earn their trust in your ability to handle the Word accurately and in your willingness to submit to it yourself. As you begin to move through Scripture in the pulpit, you'll eventually come to the passages about elders and deacons, and the implications for the current structure of the church will be more readily apparent.

Perhaps most important, relying on the power of the preached Word to instruct members about the elder/deacon model will show the congregation that these are not simply your own ideas. When you take the point of the text as the point of the sermon, your teaching simply emerges from Scripture as the clear implication for corporate life together. This is crucial. Genuinely converted Christians need to know that you are not simply calling for change in order to make your personal leadership dream a reality, but that you are following the Word in calling the congregation back to biblical fidelity in their corporate life. Expositional preaching helps you earn the congregation's trust and then allows you to present the elder-led model as Scripture's idea, not your own.

Recognition

Once the congregation has been clearly taught about the biblical basis for the elder-led model, they have motivation to look for those who might qualify as elders; and once they've been taught about the biblical qualifications for eldership, the body now has eyes to recognize who among them might fit the bill.

It makes sense for the pastor—as the only congregationally recognized elder—to be the one primarily tasked with discovering who might be qualified to become elders. He should certainly ask for informal recommendations and involvement from the congregation, and he may even be wise to form an ad hoc committee of members who help him in the discovery process. But as the congregationally recognized spiritual leader and authority among them, the pastor/elder is the one who will be tasked with the responsibility to recognize and nominate potential elders.[3]

Nomination

Once the pastor has recognized a man as potentially gifted for eldership, the man is nominated by the pastor (again, because he holds the office of elder) at the members' meeting prior to the one in which the congregation is scheduled to vote. It cannot be stressed enough that only the elders should nominate other elders, both because they are the most spiritually mature members of the congregation and because they know the lives of the congregation best. It is a personal embarrassment for a man to be nominated for eldership year after year by a member who has no idea, for instance, that that man struggles with a sin such as pornography.

Since it is likely that the pastor is the only elder, the motion to nominate will need to be seconded by another member. It is best if the nomination then rests with the congregation for about two months. This delay gives members ample time to consider the nominee and approach the pastor or elders privately—and graciously—with any concerns about the nominee's qualifications. Members intending to speak publicly in opposition to a candidate should privately express their objection to the pastor as far in advance as possible. These deliberate precautions can go a long way toward minimizing the amount of conflict in the public arena.[4]

Think Tank

1. Who is responsible for nominating elders in your church? Why? Are those biblical reasons?

2. Why is a context of consistent exposition of Scripture important for structural changes in church leadership?

Election

The congregational affirmation (election) of an elder nominee should be done at a members' meeting, ideally two months after the initial nomination, depending on the frequency of the members' meetings. All that's left is to take the congregational vote. The percentage needed for a nominee to be elected can range anywhere from 50.1 percent to 100 percent, and should be clarified in the church constitution. Choosing a percentage at the low end of the range increases the short-term likelihood of the nominee being elected. Choosing a percentage at the high end of the range increases the long-term likelihood of congregational cooperation and support.

Installation

Upon being nominated and elected, it is advisable for the new elder(s) to be installed during an upcoming Sunday morning service. Installation will simply consist of the pastor leading the new elders in taking vows appropriate to their office. A few of the other elders will then join the pastor in laying hands on the new elders and praying for them. The following is a list of vows that new elders take publicly at Capitol Hill Baptist Church (with their responses in italics):

1. Do you reaffirm your faith in Jesus Christ as your own personal Lord and Savior? *I do.*
2. Do you believe the Scriptures of the Old and New Testaments to be the Word of God, totally trustworthy, fully inspired by the Holy Spirit, the supreme, final, and the only infallible rule of faith and practice? *I do.*
3. Do you sincerely believe the Statement of Faith and Covenant of this church contain the truth taught in the Holy Scripture? *I do.*
4. Do you promise that if at any time you find yourself out of accord with any of the statements in the Statement of Faith and Covenant you will on your own initiative make known to the pastor and other elders the change which has taken place in your views since your assumption of this vow? *I do.*
5. Do you subscribe to the government and discipline of Capitol Hill Baptist Church? *I do.*
6. Do you promise to submit to your fellow elders in the Lord? *I do, with God's help.*
7. Have you been induced, as far as you know your own heart, to accept the office of elder from love of God and sincere desire to promote his glory in the gospel of his Son? *I have.*
8. Do you promise to be zealous and faithful in promoting the truths of the gospel and the purity and peace of the Church, whatever persecution or opposition may arise to you on that account? *I do, with God's help.*
9. Will you be faithful and diligent in the exercise of all your duties as elder, whether private or public, and will you endeavor by the grace of God to adorn the profession of the gospel in your manner

of life, and to walk with exemplary piety before this congregation? *I will, by the grace of God.*

10. Are you now willing to take personal responsibility in the life of this congregation as an elder to oversee the ministry and resources of the church, and to devote yourself to prayer, the ministry of the Word and the shepherding of God's flock, relying upon the grace of God, in such a way that Capitol Hill Baptist Church and the entire Church of Jesus Christ will be blessed? *I am, with the help of God.*

We then direct these questions to the congregation:

1. Do you, the members of Capitol Hill Baptist Church, acknowledge and publicly receive this man as an elder, as a gift of Christ to this church? *We do.*
2. Will you love him and pray for him in his ministry, and work together with him humbly and cheerfully, that by the grace of God you may accomplish the mission of the church, giving him all due honor and support in his leadership to which the Lord has called him, to the glory and honor of God? *We will, by the grace of God.*

Cooperation

It cannot be emphasized enough that once a congregation votes a man in as an elder, they should cooperate with and submit to his leadership joyfully. Without a sincere intention and effort to cooperate with the leadership of the church, there is no point in electing elders to lead the congregation. Unless the elders are leading in an unbiblical or sinful way, uncooperative members are simply a bane to the local church and should seek fellowship elsewhere if their presence becomes divisive.

Rotation

Scripture neither requires nor forbids either term limits or lifetime appointments for elders, so we believe churches have liberty to decide the issue as they see fit. Because an elder-qualified man still has the potential to disqualify himself from the office, and because relational dynamics among elders may change over time, we think that term limits for nonstaff eldership serve the congregation better than lifetime appointments to the office. As a matter of prudence, our church has found it useful to appoint a man to the office of elder for three years. This particular amount of time has proven long enough for establishing continuity in leadership while building in a period of rest for each nonstaff elder. Regular rotation gives an elder enough time to develop a healthy sense of owning the responsibilities of eldership while protecting him from an overdeveloped sense of territoriality. One of the most important benefits of regular rotation is that it motivates the congregation to see more leaders developed who can take the place of those who rotate out. This protects the congregation from overdependence on only a few nonstaff leaders and promotes a healthy growth of leadership that is proportional to whatever numerical growth the Lord may be pleased to grant.

According to our current practice, each nonstaff elder may serve two consecutive terms, but must take a one-year sabbatical after two consecutive terms and must then be renominated by the elders and reaffirmed by the congregation if he is to serve a third term. Staff elders, however, are not required to take a one-year sabbatical, nor are they subject to reaffirmation after six years, since their livelihood depends on their work as elders. Again, Scripture leaves room for a diversity of practice on the matter, but this particular rotation system serves our congregation well.

Conclusion

Recognizing and electing elders to lead the church is a great privilege—the church is the apple of God's eye and, as the depository of the gospel, is the center of his redemptive plan for the universe. Electing elders is also a weighty responsibility, because in doing so we are placing people as leaders in the most spiritually important institution in the world. It only makes sense, then, that we are careful to be biblical and wise in how we go about the process so that instead of causing unnecessary friction or division among the flock of God, our method leads the flock into the green pastures of the Word and by the still waters of peaceable fellowship.

19

Staffing

BEFORE WE MOVE ON to talking about what happens when the elders gather, it might be wise to stop and think about a related leadership issue—how to go about adding staff positions and personnel.

As you preach the gospel faithfully, calling for repentance and belief week in and week out, it will not be surprising to see God blessing his Word as it goes out from your mouth over the years. He may not bring thousands upon thousands, and he may not do it as immediately as you'd prefer; but his Word never comes back void, and one implication may be increased numbers of people coming to hear the gospel preached regularly and becoming members of the church. When that time comes—when God sovereignly chooses to draw more people to hear his Word and become members of the local church—you will need other full-time workers to help you reap the harvest and shepherd the growing flock responsibly.

How will you go about bringing them in? What staff positions will you create first? Why? What kind of people are you looking to bring in, how will you organize them, and why will you do things this way?

Why Not Specialize?

One of the most popular ways of hiring and organizing a church staff has been to divide the variegated lump of ministry responsibilities into specialized departments such as music, youth, adult education, community, evangelism, discipleship, and the like. It only makes sense, then, to look for a person who is particularly suited or gifted to lead in one of those areas. So we hire a minister of music or youth, a director of adult education, a pastor of evangelism, and so on. And if we really hit the jackpot, we'll get a two-for-one—a pastor of evangelism *and* discipleship!

Now if you happen to be a pastor who has organized his staff in precisely this way, let me preface my comments by first saying that there is not anything necessarily wrong with this way of doing things. Nowhere does the Bible forbid specialized ministry departments. But is specialization best for the leaders and the congregation?

Think Tank

1. *Stop reading!* What do you think? Are there dangers to be avoided in staff specialization?

2. If your staff is specialized, are you taking precautions to avoid those dangers?

3. If you've not yet hired staff members, can you think of an alternative staff structure?

Professionalization. The idea of specializing comes primarily from the professional world. The professional who specializes in one particular aspect of his larger field is in many ways more valuable and marketable than a generalist. The specialist concentrates on doing one thing and becoming known for doing it well. The better he does that one thing, the better known he becomes and the more lucrative his enterprise; and no one would argue that there's anything necessarily wrong with specialization in a secular profession. It's simply how things often work. So we have all kinds of doctors, lawyers, communication consultants, and so on who have carved out their own niches in the market, some of whom are actually strong Christians with godly motivations. And when we ourselves need a pediatrician or a civil-rights lawyer, we're grateful for their services, because they are, after all, "the experts."

It is easy to import this "professional specialist" mentality into the church. In one sense, all you have to do is change the language from "specialization and career" to "gifting and call." But vocational ministry in the church is not just another secular profession. Yes, there is a sense in which we want to do most what we're most gifted to do. God places each part in the body just as he desires. But it is equally true that every member of the church should be willing to serve where he is most needed, not always just where he is most gifted. I may be the associate pastor, but if there's a dire need for nursery workers, I shouldn't be above serving once a month, whether children's ministry is in my "gift mix" or not.

Ministry, then, should not be niche marketed. In fact, it shouldn't be marketed at all. But the effect of specialization is the introduction of a professionalized, market-driven mentality to ministry. In other words, as soon as we say we need to fill the niche of "youth minister," we have already revealed that we think the solution to our youth problem is to hire a professional who specializes in youth. On the other side of the equation, the impulse is for potential job candidates to view themselves as niche-marketed ministers who are specially equipped to fill these kinds of gaps. This niche marketing of ministers in turn encourages them to become overly narrow in their church involvement and service. Instead of becoming well-rounded and willing to serve wherever the need arises in the church, the niche minister is encouraged to confine his sphere of influence and service to the specialized niche for which he was hired. If he continues to do his job well in the specialized ministry he's paid to perform, then it is often tacitly assumed that he is a mature, growing Christian, when in fact his growth may be truncated by the narrowness of his ministry focus. Yet vocational ministers are held up as models for the congregation, and thus the congregation's idea of Christian maturity gets truncated as well. This simply cannot be the healthiest way to encourage vocational ministers to think about themselves, their service to the church, or Christian maturity.

Fragmentation. The professional nature of specialization naturally tends to insert professional space between pastor and pastor, and between the members of the congregation.

Under a more general paradigm of ministry, the pastors are more noticeably working together, side by side, in serving the church. Specialization tends to enclose pastors in their own ministry cubicles, as it were, each working only on the projects that pertain to his own niche, often coming together for little more than a perfunctory staff meeting and prayer. No longer are deep pastoral relationships being built in the shoulder-to-shoulder trench work of the ministry. The work has all been parsed into separate departments. As such, pastoral ministry becomes unhelpfully alienating. The togetherness and consequent fellowship of the pastoral staff team is compromised right from the outset.

The professional space between the members of the congregation becomes evident when those involved in one ministry or program become polarized from those in other ministries. Take, for example, the youth ministry. Simply by specializing the youth, we're separating them from the adults. But aren't we trying to train them to become adults? So why are we taking them away from the very sources of influence that can help them grow up? We're doing it, often, because we've professionally specialized our ministries to make them look more marketable to our "target audience." And so adults pass teenagers in the hallways like ships in the night, never dreaming that each could build up the other. Choir members are kept so busy with the music program that they are made almost completely unavailable for child-care ministries or service to the elderly. Devotees of the evangelism program begin to look down on others who are not equally committed to coming out on Tuesday nights. All the while, the pastor of discipleship and theological development is tempted to think that singing the songs at church isn't really his bag, so he just endures it until he can enjoy the real action in the sermon. Yet each one thinks that because he is so deeply involved in a specialized ministry, he has arrived at spiritual maturity, seldom considering or perhaps even noticing the deterioration of the adjoining ligaments that (used to) hold the corporate body together. The body falls apart, but few know, or even wonder, why.

Territoriality. Under a more general paradigm of ministry, all the pastors share all the ministry. Cultivating this healthy sense of shared ownership is good. But the fragmentation that specialized ministries introduce often leads pastors to become possessive over their particular area of service. Subtle bitterness and resentments begin to develop when lines are tested or crossed; and turf wars over music or counseling gradually become par for the course primarily because each pastor begins to think of a certain area of ministry as "my domain," and the decisions made in that area as falling under "my jurisdiction."

Program drivenness. Specialized ministry positions sometimes lead to a dependence on programs to make ministries succeed. Instead of seeing the corporate ministry of the church as a unified whole, specialized ministers almost naturally become myopic—they develop tunnel vision that's focused on only part of the whole. When "their" part seems to be malfunctioning, the only solutions they can see are localized, because the separation of departments has blinded them to the possibility that the problem in their area might be caused by a problem in a different but connected area. For example, "Our evangelism isn't efficient, so we must need a program to help us." Perhaps. But could it be that our evangelism isn't working because the discipleship is so absent that the church's witness in the community has been tainted by the hypocrisy of the members?

In another sense, this program drivenness ends up being another brand of professionalization of ministry.[1] Taking a program-oriented approach to evangelism, discipleship, or music ends up communicating to the congregation, however unintentionally, that maturity in that particular discipline of the Christian life means involvement in the current program used by the church. The truth of the matter is that involvement in the program may just be the beginning. Maturity is a godly *lifestyle*, not just attendance at a weekly event.

What's the Alternative?

So there are some good (albeit pragmatic) reasons to be skeptical about the wisdom of establishing specialized ministry positions as we think about developing a full-time pastoral staff. Stated positively, retaining a more general paradigm of ministry cultivates unity among the pastoral staff, reduces the chance of ministry being perceived as a professional career, and minimizes the splintering of ministries, pastoral teams, and congregations. But it seems that specialized ministry is almost all there is out there. So what do we do now?

An all-around ministry. What we want to work toward is a staff model that contributes to the integration of ministries, the evangelical camaraderie of pastors, and the unity of church members. Of course, this has implications for how we structure the ministries of the church. It means that we resist the temptation to break all the aspects of pastoral ministry into respective departmental heads: no more Music Department to be run by the minister of music; no more Youth Department, Evangelism Department, or Adult Education Department. Forget about departments! Departments entail divisions, and divisions simply are not helpful for the church.

"Well, how in the world are we supposed to get anything done without departments?" It may be best to present a vision of pastoral ministry as a corporate unity, an integrated, indivisible whole. There are, of course, still different aspects of that whole. But as we organize the ministries of the church, we don't attempt to do so by highlighting and then institutionalizing those differences into departments. Instead, we want to view pastoral ministry (and, by extension, Christian maturity) as one integrated unit with distinguishable parts that grow together in proportion to the whole. This way, there is no "department" to become possessive about, and there are no hard and fast lines between ministries. It's all fluid, integrated—one body.

How then does this general vision of an integrated ministry get worked out in life and get staffed with people? Here's a suggestion based on what we've seen happen at our church.

Versatile players. Instead of hiring specialists, we've found it useful to hire pastoral staff members who are willing to be generalists.

1. *Pastoral assistants.* If the church you serve is small or just getting started, chances are the budget isn't very big, so you may not be able to afford a full-fledged associate pastor just yet. That's okay. Hire pastoral assistants (PAs). The pastoral-assistant position is a full-time temporary assignment (usually lasting one or two years) filled by a man who may or may not be recognized by the congregation as gifted and called for full-time pastoral ministry. The PA serves at the will of the senior pastor, which usually means doing anything from drafting correspondence and making travel arrangements to discipling other men, preaching periodically, making hospital visits, writing curriculum, assimilating people into small groups, and observing elders' meetings.

The best PAs are usually single, postundergraduate, preseminary guys who are thinking about entering pastoral ministry and who want to test their gifts in the context of the local church.[2] They can usually live on a lot less than a husband and father of two, and they will usually appreciate (or at least not mind) living in church housing.

This assistantship, then, can actually double as a pastoral apprenticeship or training program, especially if you as a pastor are deliberate about giving them good reading materials, meeting with them periodically to do them spiritual good, observing them do ministry, and giving them constructive feedback as they get their feet wet. These guys won't be considered full-fledged pastors in the staffing sense, but they'll be able to do a lot of the legwork that helps you push the pastoral ministry forward. And they may even have the character and willingness to serve as elders.

The PA position trains young men to be generalists in ministry. It helps them to develop a well-rounded pastoral repertoire of experience by allowing them to do a variety of things that build up the church and push pastoral ministry forward. As such, it works toward correcting the specialized view of pastoral ministry by replacing it with a more robust model of pastoral and spiritual maturity. In short, it trains guys to play every position.

If your budget allows only enough money for one PA, that's okay. Bring in a promising prospect, let the church see the value of his ministry and of the training he's getting from you, and try to cultivate a corporate sense of the importance of building into the lives of aspiring pastors so that the budget line for PAs can gradually grow.

2. *Assistant pastors.* These are not to be confused with pastoral assistants. Pastoral assistants can often be called from outside the congregation, are not considered staff pastors, and may or may not be elected to the office of elder. Assistant pastors, in our practice, are called only from within the congregation, are recognized by the congregation as gifted and called for the full-time ministry of preaching and teaching, and are acknowledged as elders by virtue of their recognized character and call.

Assistant pastors, then, assist the senior and/or associate pastor(s) in the performance of their duties and perform various other duties pertaining to the pastoral office. While assistant pastors may be given responsibility for the general oversight of a certain area of ministry (unlike pastoral assistants), they are not called "ministers of" that particular area, and their responsibilities often range outside the confines of that particular area. So an assistant pastor may be entrusted with oversight of children's ministry but would also be called upon to disciple other men, preach, do hospital visitation, officiate at weddings or funerals, and the like.

The assistant pastors are, in this way, trained to play every position, which reduces the likelihood of fragmentation and territoriality, and protects the congregation from becoming overly dependent on any one staff person, including the senior pastor. These men should be paid more than pastoral assistants, primarily because they are more qualified in both character and ability, and so are given more responsibility.

3. *Associate pastors.* Ideally, as the church and its budget grow, it will be wise to work toward bringing in a full-fledged associate pastor. Often we think of an associate as someone who has different gifts than the senior pastor so that he can do the work that the senior man is less gifted at. This seems wise at first blush but in the end may prove a bit shortsighted.

As Protestants, we want to discourage the congregation from depending too much on the person and ministry of the senior pastor. Granted, he is probably there because he has pronounced gifts of preaching, teaching, and leadership. But if something were to happen to him, or if the relationship between the congregation and the senior pastor were to become sour, then there would be no one of similar gifting to take up the banner if the associate was hired precisely because his gifts were different. It's always good to have more than one person on the boat who can steer the ship.

For this reason, it may be wise to hire an associate pastor whose gifts and call are very similar to the senior pastor's but who is willing to put himself under the senior pastor's authority and serve in similar yet complementary ways.

The Relationships between Staff, Elders, and Deacons

We would encourage churches to keep a healthy distinction between the role of the elders and the role of the staff. We often say that our church is elder led but staff executed. The elders work together to determine the spiritual direction of the church, and the staff members work together to fulfill the vision or direction set corporately by the elders.

Of course, some staff members will also be elders in most situations—at the very minimum, the senior pastor will be an elder, and so will an associate pastor (if there is one). Staff members who are also elders, then, are responsible both for setting the vision of the church (as elders) and for implementing that vision (as staff). Staff members who are not also elders are not responsible for setting the vision or direction of the church. They are simply responsible for carrying out their part of the vision set by the elders. The elders decide where the church goes, because they are the men whom the congregation has recognized as having the spiritual maturity to make those kinds of decisions. The staff members drive the bus in order to get us all there, because they are the ones who are released from secular employment to minister full time and equip the saints for the work of ministry.

Deacons make sure we have enough gas to get to where we're going.[3] They release the elders to devote themselves to spiritual leadership by serving in physical and financial matters in a way that brings unity among the church under the authority of the elders (Acts 6:1–6). In our church, we create deacon positions according to the practical needs of the body. So we currently have a deacon for each of the following areas: budget, bookstall, building accessibility, library, sound, child care, children's ministry, children's ministry recruitment, ordinances, member care, hospitality, ushers, weddings, community outreach, college ministry, international outreach, parking, welcome team, youth ministry, and media. Whenever a need arises that seems to require special attention or the need to coordinate volunteers, we feel the freedom to create a deacon position and look for a member whose current service and character are particularly suited to the task. Conversely, whenever a deacon position seems to outlive its usefulness, we feel free to discontinue the position as a way of conserving the energy of the body and pruning the ministry branches that are either no longer needed or are no longer bearing fruit.[4]

The elders decide on the destination. The staff members drive the bus. The deacons make sure we've got enough gas to get there.

Conclusion

Staffing a church may seem like a pretty mundane thing to think about. In fact, we might even be tempted to think that staffing decisions are part of the business end of the church and don't really affect the spiritual health of the body. Hopefully we've seen that to be far from the truth. A staff configuration that promotes the health of the church begins with a healthy concept of shared pastoral ministry. If we begin by thinking about shared pastoral ministry in a specialized, fragmented way, we are setting up both the staff and the church to become fragmented along those same lines. Conversely, wise decisions made during the staffing process can actually serve the church in encouraging and edifying ways that promote the unity and proportional growth of the body.

If you are in a small church at the beginning stages of a reforming work, think before you staff! Be deliberate about *how* you build your staff structure—*who* you bring onto the pastoral staff and *why* you do things that way. Think rigorously and biblically about the implications of your staff configuration for the pastoral team's concept of a healthy ministry and for the congregation's concept of spiritual maturity.

These precautions may seem constraining now, but as your church grows under the faithful exposition of the Word, they will free both the pastors and the members to become much more well rounded in their vocational ministries, in their personal church involvement, and in their understanding of Christian maturity. As the corporately held understanding of mature membership and ministry becomes fuller over time, the corporate testimony of the church will begin to shine all the more brightly in the community. The flame won't be contained under the bushel for too long.

Recommended Reading for Section 3

ON FINDING ELDERS

Anyabwile, Thabiti. *Finding Faithful Elders and Deacons* (Wheaton, IL: Crossway, 2012).

Dever, Mark. *Understanding Church Leadership* (Nashville: B&H, 2012).

Dickson, David. *The Elder and His Work* (Phillipsburg, NJ: P&R, 2004).

Leeman, Jonathan. *The Rule of Love: How the Local Church Should Reflect God's Love and Authority* (Wheaton, IL: Crossway, 2018).

Leeman, Jonathan. *Understanding the Congregation's Authority* (Nashville: B&H, 2016).

Menikoff, Aaron. *Character Matters* (Chicago: Moody, 2020).

Newton, Phil, and Matt Schmucker. *Elders in the Life of the Church: Rediscovering the Biblical Model for Church Leadership* (Grand Rapids, MI: Kregel, 2014).

Piper, John. *Biblical Eldership* (Minneapolis: Desiring God Ministries, 1999).

SECTION 4

WHEN THE ELDERS GATHER

20

The Word and Prayer

LEADERSHIP MEETINGS. Do you look forward to them? Do you look forward to leading them? Some of us have had such adversarial experiences in church leadership meetings that we've soured on the idea of being so close to the action. Grazed by a verbal bullet once too often, we're not always sure we want to jump back in just to take another one in the breadbasket. Others of us have entered leadership meetings only to feel as if we've jumped headfirst into a puddle of ignorance. Both experiences make us wonder at times if there's anything at all that can redeem the church leadership meeting.

In the last section, we dealt with the process of gathering elders. That process can help weed out potentially immature members who are likely to make elders' meetings less than pleasurable. In this section, we want to reflect for a moment on what elders should be doing when they get together, and how to go about doing it.

But why meet together as elders in the first place? After all, Paul never commands Timothy or Titus to convene elder meetings fortnightly, and Acts 15 is regional, not just local. Yet the biblical model of plural eldership (Acts 14:23), combined with the nature of the pastoral task—caring for the sheep, counseling them, overseeing them, leading them, praying for them, protecting them—often gives rise to the meeting of the shepherds as a prudent method to decide how we might best guide and guard the flock together.

Of course, most of our eldering activity happens outside our meetings—while we're actually with the sheep! That's as it should be. Shepherds don't just talk about sheep, we smell like them. But it's simply not possible for every elder to know every sheep equally well. That being the case, meeting together is a way for us to pool together our relational knowledge of the congregation so that we can pray more pointedly, counsel more effectively, and decide more wisely. What's more, our direct contact with the sheep will often raise questions for individual elders that are best discussed and answered in a prayerful gathering of the shepherds.

So while elder meetings are not commanded in Scripture, neither are they forbidden; and for many elder teams, they're a useful tool that facilitates wise and harmonious oversight together.

Our elders meet together every other week, usually on a Thursday evening. You may choose to meet more or less frequently. But regardless of how often you meet, the most important thing to establish among the elders is unity around God's Word. If we want the unity of our church to be fundamentally built on the Word, then the unity of our elders must be built on the Word.

The Word

Reading it. A typical elders' meeting at Capitol Hill Baptist starts with reading the Bible. Beginning with Bible reading reorients the elders from themselves to God and each other; from their own ideas to God's ideas; from the business philosophy that runs the companies they work for to the principles of godliness that govern the church. It calls elders to renew their minds together in Scripture, forging unity among them. It also functions to remind the elders that as they exercise a measure of authority in making decisions on behalf of the church, they too sit under the authority of the Word. Elders are called to submit to God's Word no less than the rest of the sheep in God's flock. Hearing the Word read reminds them that their authority is not their own but is derived from God's Word. This reading, then, helps the elders recognize that God's Word deserves primacy in the conversation, which in turn cultivates humility—a most necessary quality to display when conducting the spiritual affairs of the church.

Normally, the elders will read the passage that is to be preached on the following Sunday. As they read, they will be looking for aspects of God's character or work for which to praise and thank him. This is important. It's not mindless or unreflective reading, but thoughtful reading that is looking for reasons in the text to praise and thank God. This way of reading God's Word makes a difference, because it begins to change our attitudes toward the Word, God, and each other. Instead of complaining, we're looking to praise God and give him thanks. Instead of assuming that whatever we say will please God, we're coming to be taught by the text how to praise God in a pleasing way.

Praying it. Once the elders have read through the passage to be preached the next Sunday, they pray through it. Having picked from the text some divine attribute for which to praise God, or some grace that he has conferred on us that draws us out to him in adoration, each elder will pray a one- or two-sentence prayer of praise. This is part of how the elders are being intentional about devoting themselves to prayer and the ministry of the Word (Acts 6:1–4).

Studying it. Periodically an issue will arise in the congregation that requires some biblical study on the part of the elders. Don't waste these opportunities! These can be some of the richest and most rewarding times in the life of an elder body. As circumstances in the congregation raise biblical and theological questions, use these occasions to give the elders experience in searching the Scriptures together. Provide them with study tools, such as commentaries or good theological books on a particular topic. Encouraging the elders in this direction will not only augment their biblical knowledge but will also show them what it looks like to shepherd a flock of God's people in a theologically aware, biblically responsible way.

Such study will also be beneficial for the congregation, especially as the elders make the fruits of their study known to the body in the form of a summary document that presents the biblical position the elders have taken on the matter.

This kind of study is an important part of the elders' corporate spiritual leadership of the flock. This is part of how the shepherds of the church lead the flock into the green pastures of applied theology. Too often we complain that our congregations simply aren't interested in theology. But why should they be if they aren't led to be by their elders? The study of the elders and the presentation of their biblical conclusions can help develop the theological appetite of the congregation as they see their leaders taking theology seriously and applying it faithfully to the corporate life of the church. As a result, strategic study of the Bible conducted among the elders on issues concerning the life of their local church can have the effect of developing the theological maturity and discernment of the members. This is where we want to lead God's flock—into the pastures of his Word.

Think Tank

1. Read 2 Kings 22:8–23:14. What preceded the reforms instituted by King Josiah? Why was it important that Josiah keep this in view as he went about his work as king? What was the ultimate result of Judah's longstanding disobedience to God's Word (see 23:26–27)?

2. Read Nehemiah 8:13–18. What prompted renewed obedience to the law of God among the leaders? Why had they been disobedient for so long?

3. How do you conduct your leaders'/elders' meetings? Why do you do it that way?

4. How might reading and praying Scripture change the tone of your meetings? How might it work toward changing the maturity and spiritual atmosphere of your church?

Prayer

For each other. After the Word has been read and prayed through, the elders will share with each other what's going on in their lives—concerns at work or home, spiritual struggles, personal relationships, answered prayers, and so forth. This time of sharing provides a measure of accountability and mutual encouragement that's crucial to the integrity and longevity of any elder's ministry. It functions as a regular opportunity for the elders to express care for one another, to monitor one another's spiritual health, and to reaffirm relational trust among each other. Faithfulness here can go a long way toward combating pastoral isolation and cultivating meaningful spiritual relationships characterized by mutual humility and love. Once everyone has had an opportunity to share, each elder prays for another. This may seem like an obvious step to some, but many elder bodies neglect prayer and treat their gatherings more like meetings of corporate executives rather than meetings of God's undershepherds.

For individual church members. One of the most strategic times for elders to pray for other members is during elders' meetings. Perhaps you won't be able to pray for every single member of your church during this part of the meeting. But you can make a habit of having the elders take turns praying one- or two-sentence prayers for a few people on each page of the church directory, or perhaps praying more thoroughly through one section of it. Even if you don't know every person all that well, this practice will encourage you to get to know them personally so that you can pray for them more specifically, and it will give elders practice in praying simple biblical prayers for others. Praying for the sheep together as a gathered group of undershepherds is an excellent way to promote the spiritual health of the congregation, to keep each other as elders accountable to faithfulness in prayer for the congregation, and to lead by example.

For the corporate body. It's tempting to think that we should just pray that God would make our churches bigger. But what we're really after is health, not just size. Churches can be incredibly unhealthy even when they're big. A small, healthy church is better than a big, unhealthy church. That's right. A bigger church isn't always a better church. It may make us look better as leaders, but size doesn't always indicate health (as so many of our bodies attest!). So it makes sense to stop and ask yourself: What are your motives for praying as you do for your church? When we gather as a group of elders, we need to be praying not just that God would make our church bodies bigger, but that he would make them healthier. Memorizing Paul's prayers for the churches would be a great start for a group of elders. Encourage your elders over the coming weeks to memorize Ephesians 1:15–23; 3:16–19; Philippians 1:9–11; Colossians 1:9–14; 1 Thessalonians 3:11–13; and 2 Thessalonians 1:11–12. Lead by example, and pray that these qualities and habits would be characteristic of and increasing in the corporate life and testimony of your church.

Here's a list of general, biblical prayers you can pray for the whole local church, in no particular order. You might consider putting it in the front or back of your own membership directory and encouraging both the elders and the congregation to pray a few of these a day. It can also be a useful reference for the elders during prayer together at elder meetings.

Pray that we would preserve our unity even in our diversity as a witness to the gospel's uniting power (Eph. 4:2).

Pray for a local revival of godly sorrow, conviction, and spiritual interest in the Bible.

Pray that God would create a new local appetite for expositional preaching of the Bible.

Pray for good fruit from the regular preaching of God's Word in the local church.

Pray that all members would look out for each other's interests (Phil. 2:5–7).

Pray that the elders would equip the saints for the work of ministry (Eph. 4:11–12).

Pray that members would be faithful to make disciples, to build a culture of discipleship, and to see disciple making as part of what it means to be a Christian (Matt. 28:18–20; 2 Tim. 2:2).

Pray for growth in the church's ability to encourage and counsel one another from Scripture.

Pray that established members would be hospitable to newer members, visitors, and those different from themselves.

Pray that the congregation would welcome political, economic, social, and racial diversity as God gives it.

Pray for growth in personal holiness, love, and faithfulness.

Pray for Christ to be honored in our work and that we would commend the gospel to others in our words and conduct during the week.

Pray that the congregation would grow in prioritizing attendance at the public meetings of the church.

Pray for growing maturity in giving and receiving godly criticism and encouragement.

Pray for the children of members to become obedient to their parents in the Lord.

Pray that the church's reach for the gospel would broaden to more people and places.

Pray for growth in a gracious and patient attitude toward those who disagree with us.

Pray that God would give the congregation more good purposes to spread the gospel and do good (2 Thess. 1:11).

Pray for growing faithfulness and fruitfulness in private Bible reading.

Pray for growing faithfulness in private prayer for each other.

Pray for God to deepen the congregation's relationships with each other to center on encouragement, confession, and gospel ministry.

Pray for maturity in being slow to take offense and quick to receive correction.

Pray that the elders would watch their life and doctrine closely (1 Tim. 4:16).

Pray that the congregation would bear fruit in every way and increase in the knowledge of God with gratitude (Col. 1:9–12).

Pray for growth in a shared heart for personal, local evangelism (Acts 8:4).

Pray for growth in a shared heart for international missions and that the Lord would raise up more workers for his harvest (Matt. 9:38; Acts 1:8).

Pray for fruitful Bible-reading friendships between us and our non-Christian friends.

Pray that God would raise up additional qualified elders, preachers, evangelists, and deacons among us (Acts 13:1–3).

Pray for good fruit from the ministries of the elders and deacons.

Pray for good fruit from the men's and women's discipling relationships in the church.

Think Tank

1. Read Ephesians 3:16–19. What makes this such a good prayer to pray for a local church?

2. Read Colossians 1:9–14. Try to memorize this passage by reciting it and praying it once a day for three weeks. Memorize another prayer passage each week for a month. Reinforce it in your mind and heart by praying it daily and repeatedly for other leaders and members of your church.

Conclusion

There are plenty of ways to grow a big church really fast. But God has promised to bring healthy life and growth to his church by his Word and by his Spirit. Making a firm commitment to Bible reading and prayer in elders' meetings, then, is to put ourselves in the stream of the only real sources of power that God has unequivocally promised to bless. As we carry out this commitment to the Word and prayer among the gathered elders, we will be encouraging the congregation to trust not in programs or personalities, not in advertisements or physical amenities, but rather in the powerful Word of God and in the promise of his life-giving Spirit.

21

The Agenda: What to Talk About

NOW THAT THE ELDERS have read the Word, shared each other's burdens and joys, and prayed for one another and for the church, what else should happen when they meet? What should godly elders do when they get together?

Preparation

One of the problems that usually needs to be overcome in elders' meetings is the disparity of knowledge between staff and nonstaff elders. Simply because it is their job to be dealing with pastoral situations day in and day out, staff elders will usually come into an elders' meeting having thought about the issues for discussion quite a bit more than elders with full-time secular vocations. The other staff and I used to come into the meetings having already thought or talked for hours about certain pastoral matters, and the nonstaff elders were right to point out that it was a little unfair to expect them to form opinions and make decisions on the same matters in fifteen minutes or less!

So we started writing and distributing the agenda to the nonstaff elders a week in advance, complete with explanatory memos attached. This way the nonstaff elders were given time to read up on the items for conversation, think through them a bit on their own, and pray about them before they were actually called upon to share their thoughts. This was one of the most helpful changes we had made in our procedure to that point, because it enabled the nonstaff elders to be briefed ahead of time and to be more ready to engage on the same level as the staff. It narrowed the knowledge gap between staff and nonstaff elders, it made the nonstaff elders feel more a part of the conversation, it enabled the nonstaff elders to contribute with more wisdom, it headed off any potential rift between staff and nonstaff elders, and it made our meetings a lot more productive.

Prepare and distribute elder packets a week in advance. This will require all the elders to have any memos written a week ahead of time as well, so make sure that expectation is clear. It will also require confidentiality—the last thing you want is potentially sensitive material lying around the church for just anyone to pick up and read. We've found that it's best to staple the elder packet together (agenda on top, then a membership report, a financial report, and all relevant memos) and place it in a sealed envelope with the elder's name on it.

Categories for Conversation

Reading the Bible and praying will usually take us between one-and-a-half and two hours. This may seem like a lot of time, but remember—these are the things to which elders are supposed to be devoting themselves (Acts 6:4). At this point, we'll take a break, and then come back to discuss the spiritual business of the church. Here are our operating categories. Of course, you may choose different ones, or tweak the ones we've presented here. But this is how it works best for us. The two overarching categories for our elder conversations are *principial matters* and *pastoral matters*.

Principial matters have to do with theological or ethical principles—not specific situations, but rather doctrinal, moral, or ministry topics on which we'd like to come to a common mind. These are topics such as the mission of the church, any point of our statement of faith, marriage and divorce, complementarianism, transgenderism, racism in the church, or whether to organize the congregation according to a parish system. On ministry topics in particular, this is our opportunity to ask, "What should we think of this kind of situation when it arises, and how should we normally address it?"

We'll normally read a good book together on the topic to facilitate our conversation. Often it's a book we agree with and want to use as a good model, but we'll also read books we know we disagree with from time to time so as to keep abreast of modern currents and sharp in how we interact with error. These are conversations that further equip, establish, and unify the elders in sound doctrine and practice. Of course, as an elder team grows, and as particular elders rotate on and off, the composition of the team will naturally change, and the shared conclusions we reach about particular topics are revisited or revised as necessary over time.

We've learned by experience that if we don't set aside a few of our elder meetings a year for just this kind of principial conversation, all our meetings will be dominated by situational and urgent concerns among the flock, postponing the principial topics and in the process leaving the elders themselves without much ongoing training. So we've devoted at least a half dozen meetings each year to reading and discussing theological, moral, or ministry matters that will further equip us and guide our future decision-making when relevant situations arise.

We've also learned from experience that it's important for our nonstaff elders to always be included in these principial conversations. Since staff elders are often together for a significant portion of the week, it can be easy and even fun for them to talk through these principial matters in the office. But if the staff members are always coming to agreement on doctrinal, moral, or ministry principles apart from their nonstaff brother elders, that can cleave the elder team with unintentional consequences for the unity of the board as a whole.

Pastoral matters have to do with the care of particular members in the congregation. (We devote one meeting a month to such particular, pastoral concerns. Eight months of the year we have a second meeting devoted to more theological or principial topics. We call these "issues meetings.")

Skin is an important part of the human body. When it's working well, our skin keeps out harmful contaminants, it covers our muscles and veins in an attractive and comfortable way, and it keeps all our fluids in place. We don't often think about it until we get a cut. But as soon as our skin is broken, we realize how easy it is for our bodies to be infected with bacteria, or simply hurt by the pain of exposure. It's the same with the church. As elders, one of the most important things we do is tend to the skin of the local body of Christ. In other words, we are constantly asking, "Who's coming in?" and, "Who's going out?" "Have you seen Mrs. Smith lately?" and "Do you think we should admit this potential member?" We don't want to let in the harmful contaminants of unregenerate members, and we don't want to let the lifeblood of the church—her truly converted members—slip away unnoticed.

When we turn to member care in our elders' meetings, we proceed with losses, then additions, and finally the care list. First, we tend to those members whom we have lost due to resignation of their membership, death, or church discipline. Then we tend to prospective new members. As the senior pastor, I will typically present the testimony of each prospective new member that I've interviewed and will submit their names to the other elders for recommendation to the congregation as new members.

Finally, we tend to the care list. The care list is simply an informal list of people whom the elders have recognized as needing special attention for a variety of reasons. Periodically a person is put on the care list because of a particularly extreme kind of trial. More often, though, the care list is used to keep track of those people whom the elders have noticed as being delinquent in attendance over the course of a few months[1] or as being involved in scandalous sin that will require church discipline if not repented of quickly. Putting someone on the care list is part of the spiritual oversight of the elders, and as such does not require a vote by the congregation.

How does it work? Usually an elder has contacted (or has at least attempted to contact) the member in question, often more than once, to talk about the particular issue at hand. The rest of the members are simply notified, at the next members' meeting, as to who is on the care list and why. This gives elders a few weeks until the following members' meeting to talk with those who are on the care list and try to shepherd them back closer to the fold. If those on the care list do not respond, they are removed from membership at the next members' meeting (usually held every two months). Notifying the rest of the members in advance about the names on the care list also allows everyone to be made aware of the situation so that a person's removal from membership comes as less of a surprise and causes less of a stir. It also allows the body to do its work, because the first point of contact with a care-list member is usually from a member who has a natural relationship with him.

Our practice is to put the additions, resignations, and members to be removed all on a single sheet of paper, along with a note regarding total membership prior to additions and potential membership should all additions pass. This document constitutes our Membership Report, which is part of every elders' packet and central to every elders' meeting.

Depending on how static or dynamic your membership is, it can be quite challenging to stay abreast of all the changes that are happening in the lives of your members. The composition of your flock may be changing drastically right under your nose. But if you don't know all the sheep very well, or if you're not diligent to guard the gate, then it's easy for wolves to slip in unnoticed or for sheep to slip away without comment. Yet the pastor will in some sense give an account to God for the souls entrusted to his care (Heb. 13:17).

This is why a plurality of elders is so crucial to responsible shepherding. Other elders can help the senior pastor keep an eye out for who's been faithfully attending and who's been lax, who's moving out of the area, and who's been deployed overseas. One of the ways we as elders try to stay on top of membership issues is to go through two or three letters of the alphabet in the membership directory during each elders' meeting, asking each other about the spiritual condition of each person and whether any of the elders have had informative conversations that might be helpful for shepherding purposes. Pastorally, then, you'll need to ask members to make sure they let you know when they're moving or when they're deployed out of the area so that you and the other elders can make the requisite changes to the membership rolls.

It will also be helpful on this front to revise the church membership directory monthly, or at least quarterly, depending on how much your membership changes. I understand how paper-intensive this commitment can be. But it is the best way we know of to keep up with who's in, who's out, and who's just out of town.

Think Tank

1. Why is it important for elders to talk about issues of membership, member care, and discipline?

2. How often do you and the other leaders of your church talk about membership issues like these?

3. What are some practical steps you can take to be more diligent about protecting the health and purity of your church's membership?

Beyond principial and pastoral matters, the elders deal with a number of other categories.

Administration. It's tempting to think that since the elders are to devote themselves primarily to spiritual oversight, issues regarding finances and facilities are always "deacon work." But it's important to remember that the spiritual vision and direction set by the elders gets enfleshed on the physical and financial level. So while the elders should probably not be regularly discussing janitorial performance, they are particularly wise to give periodic attention to big-picture administrative issues such as major renovations, building purchases, or budgetary concerns. So each elders' meeting will at least include a brief look at the monthly church budget, a year-to-date financial report that compares budgeted numbers with actual numbers, and a current notation of assets and liabilities. This kind of regular "look under the hood" gives the elders an idea of whether they are on target to achieve the spiritual goals they've set and enables them to adjust on the fly if necessary.

Ministry and missions. This is where the elders work to ensure that the spiritual vision of the church is realized and that the spiritual direction of the church is maintained. A wide variety of things can be discussed under this heading. Letters from missionaries in the field are often read so that we can rejoice with them or be notified about their struggles and needs. Plans for short-term missions trips are discussed. Strategies for global missions are dreamed up. Requests for missionary support are taken. Proposals from church members regarding potential new ministries are evaluated. Benevolence requests and special needs are considered. Staff changes are thought through. Constitutional revisions are made. The agenda for the next members' meeting is adjusted and approved. Local evangelistic strategies and events are talked about. Plans for future church planting are often dreamed up and appraised. One of the most important things that happens under this heading is that the elders frequently present possible names for deacon nominations. These things and a host of others come up during this part of the meeting, and these discussions are where the seeds of evangelistic strategy and effectiveness, sown by the congregation, are often watered.

When the elders are evaluating a missionary's request for financial support, we take four factors into consideration. (1) *The strategic nature of the work.* We don't want to build on someone else's foundation. If there are already a couple hundred missionaries in Kenya, but only a precious few in India, then we are more likely to support a missionary headed to India than one headed to Kenya. (2) *Relationship to our church.* Does the person asking for financial assistance have a history with our local congregation? Has this person been a longtime member? Was he a member of the congregation before moving elsewhere for further training or study? Or is this a person whom we are just now getting to know? Have we had an opportunity to observe fruit from this person's ministry over a period of months or years? We prefer to work through existing relationships with people who have proven to be in agreement with our theology and methods over time. (3) *Amount of money already in hand.* How much money has the person already raised? (4) *Competency.* How effective do we think this missionary will be in his chosen field of ministry? Has this person displayed a fitness for ministry that would seem to indicate a future trajectory of fruitfulness in his chosen area of gospel mission?

Of course, you may not have as much to talk about here if you are not at the same time encouraging the congregation to take responsibility themselves for the spread of the gospel and the well-being of other members. This is, in part, why preaching and discipling are so important. They are the conduits that pour the fuel of the gospel into the engine of the church. They are the oil that keeps the light of the congregation's evangelistic zeal burning strong and bright. Preaching and discipling are the foods that provide energy for a healthy body to work.

You may also be in a situation where the elders are still talking about the color of the carpet or what to do about the sign out front. If this is the case, keep being intentional about gradually directing them toward more spiritual goals and gospel-oriented aspirations. Each time the elders gather, bring to the table a few questions about member care, local evangelism plans, missions strategies, future elders, or issues of the church's corporate health. Whatever you do, don't give up! Keep preaching. Keep praying. Keep discipling and developing personal relationships. Keep teaching and leading by example. The Word is powerful, and God's Spirit will not fail to bless it. Keep putting it out front, and entrust yourself and your ministry to God's Word and Spirit.

Communication. When we first transitioned from the pastor/deacon model to the elder/deacon model, our communication was seriously deficient. Sometimes before members' meetings particular deacons would be asked questions by other members regarding some issue discussed by the elders. Yet since we hadn't communicated well with the deacons, they weren't prepared to answer the questions, or they would give different answers than the elders were giving. Not good! So now, at the end of each elders' meeting, we assign each elder the responsibility of contacting one or two deacons to notify them of any relevant discussions or decisions that were made, especially regarding their particular area of ministry. The elders also meet with the deacons in leadership meetings, which happen one week before the members' meetings. This way, whether a member asks an elder or a deacon, all the officers of the church are on the same page, and everyone is more likely to give the same answers and present a united front to the congregation. We've still not mastered the art, and we fail more often than we'd like. But we're always getting better and looking for ways to improve.

Regarding communication among the elders themselves during the meeting, we have found it quite useful to encourage elders to write and submit memos for distribution beforehand concerning things they want to put on the agenda for discussion. Writing our own memos can go a long way toward clarifying our own thoughts, and reading the memos of others helps us to understand their ideas better and to edit and refine our responses before entering the meeting.

One more comment on communication. If you are the main teaching pastor of your church, I'd encourage you to do all you can to cultivate an atmosphere in which all the elders are able to give and receive godly encouragement and criticism. As the one with the most derived authority by virtue of the frequency of your Bible teaching, your example will set the pace. Be joyful. Have a sense of humor. Don't take yourself too seriously. Don't get defensive when others disagree with you. Be careful not to be autocratic or heavy-handed. Don't feel as if you have to chair every meeting. Resist feeling that you always have to have the last word, or that your suggestions always need to be implemented. Trust your fellow elders. Be willing to be voted down by them on issues that aren't central to the gospel. Be difficult to offend. In taking this kind of attitude, you will model a humility that they will be likely to emulate over time, and you will earn both the respect and the trust that you are likely to compromise with heavy-handedness. Model gentleness in speech, humor in your self-concept, and humility and reasonableness when corrected. By doing this, you will reap the benefits of having a plurality of elders to help you in the work.

Let your wisdom be godly: "the wisdom from above is first pure, then peaceable, gentle, reasonable, full of mercy and good fruits, unwavering, without hypocrisy. And the seed whose fruit is righteousness is sown in peace by those who make peace. Peacemakers who sow in peace raise a harvest of righteousness" (James 3:17–18).

Issues meetings. At Capitol Hill Baptist, we have a members-centered elders' meeting once a month and a second monthly elders' meeting in nine of the twelve months. These second elders' meetings are centered not on specific member care, but more generally on caring for the members by thinking through one theological or methodological issue per meeting. The issue is always clarified by distribution of a memo prior to the meeting and sometimes by additional reading to be completed by the time the meeting begins. One elder is then responsible to record the elders' conclusions. Here are some examples of topics we've tackled at issues meetings: Bible translations, mission of the church, the transgender issue, divorce and remarriage, women's ministry, age of baptism for children, artificial insemination, marijuana, complementarianism, Christian conscience and freedom issues, child abuse, child protection policy, sexual abuse, and racism.

Think Tank

1. Reflect on your leadership and communication styles. Are there ungodly tendencies?

2. Ask a mature member of the congregation to give you honest feedback on the way you lead—and accept it graciously.

3. What are some ways you can practice giving and receiving godly encouragement and criticism with the leaders of your church?

The Annual Budget Process

Once a year, usually in May, we devote a full elders' meeting to developing the next year's budget. It's often one of the most encouraging meetings we have all year, mainly because we get to take stock of the current state of the church and dream for the coming months. I'm sure you'll want to refine the process for your own church context, but here's how we've done it.

Before the meeting, I as the senior pastor will meet with the church administrator to review last year's budget and document any significant projected changes that we already know we'll need to take into account (e.g., facilities, taxes, renovations, staff health care, etc.). Once that's done, I'll meet with the associate pastor and the elder in charge of missions to discuss the vision and budget for local outreach and global missions (we act as an informal missions subcommittee for the elders). I'll then record the budget projections, noting how much they will increase budget percentages.

During the elders' meeting devoted to the budget, I'll have all the elders go around one by one to name areas of concern where we need to see growth in the church. I'll write these on a whiteboard, and I'll keep writing until everyone has run out of things to say. Then I'll have all the elders go around and name encouragements and praises that they see in the church. One by one, I'll write these on the board, again until no one has anything else to say. These exercises force us to stop and notice the work as a whole. They help us to think strategically. Then I have all the elders name ministries or purchases that they would like to see supported in the new budget. I'll write these on the whiteboard in the same way. When everyone's said their piece, I have all the elders pick their two highest preferences that fit the amount of money we have to work with. We then work to come to agreement on our budget-change priorities for the next year.

Once we've all expressed our opinions, the elders send the suggested budget to the deacons for them to work out the details. This is the only time of the year that all the deacons meet together. The budget is then developed by the elders and deacons over the summer, sometimes being passed back and forth between them; and when the elders are agreed, they present the budget to the congregation for approval in the fall. After the congregation has had a month to look at it and pray over it, an open budget discussion is held at a members' meeting for people to ask questions and make suggestions. The congregation is given another month to look at it and pray over it, or to make further suggestions, after which a congregational vote is taken to approve or disapprove the proposed budget.

Others in the Room

Many church leaders perceive elders' meetings to be strictly off limits to the members themselves. This may be the case when particularly sensitive matters are being discussed. So our own elder meetings usually include a thirty- to sixty-minute executive session where the elders alone, with no one else in the room, talk together about particularly sensitive matters in the lives of members or elders. This is also our opportunity to consider men as possible future elders, conversations that necessarily involve critical (though charitable) assessments of people and their character and competence.

For example, we regularly have pastoral assistants and interns sitting outside the circle of elders, just listening to what is being discussed and how it's being talked about.[2] Observation is one of the most underrated methods of learning. Many young men headed into future pastoral ministry may never be invited to observe an elders' meeting before they actually have to lead one. Perhaps some of you reading this book have been unwittingly put in just this position. If so, you know firsthand how frustrating it can be to lead in a way that you've never observed someone else leading.

As you recognize young men who have solid Christian character, demonstrate public teaching gifts, are initiating with other individual members for their spiritual good, and are active in the corporate life of the church, invite them to observe the elders' meetings.[3] Let them know that they should do so silently. But let them know that it might be a good opportunity for them to see what it looks like for a group of godly men to lead spiritually and discuss matters that touch the direction and vision of the local church. Having a good model to follow is half of developing a biblically faithful way of doing ministry as an aspiring pastor. If we want to stem the tide of pragmatism, providing biblically faithful models for younger men to observe will be part of the way forward.

22

Decision-Making: How to Talk about It

THE MOST HEATED AND DIVISIVE moments in a church's life often come at critical decision-making moments. I've seen churches split because the pastor doesn't know how to advocate a conviction or method with humility, or because he doesn't react graciously when others disagree with him. It's also common for nonstaff leaders to be so entrenched in their opinions or influential positions that they end up bringing more harm than good to the decision-making table. These problems, of course, have to do in large part with the character of the men. But problems in decision-making also have to do with how leaders view the responsibility and privilege of leadership.

We've already discussed what to talk about in an elders' meeting. Now we need to think more biblically about how we talk about those matters, and how we understand and contribute to the decision-making process.

The Pastor's Role

Some pastors relish the role of chairing the elders' meeting, while others loathe it. The truth of the matter is that the senior pastor doesn't necessarily need to chair all the elders' meetings. In fact, it is probably healthy to rotate chair responsibilities yearly or every other year.

One of the healthiest by-products of the senior pastor not chairing the elders' meetings is that it communicates to all the other elders that the pastor isn't out for some sort of power grab and that he doesn't view the pastorate as a CEO position. Pastors who feel that they have to chair every elders' meeting communicate something about their own character and leadership style. It simply is not good for the elders as a body if the pastor feels threatened by allowing someone else among them to lead or if he believes that Scripture teaches that he must chair the meeting in order to lead properly.

The healthiest way for a pastor to view himself in the elders' meetings is as a sort of first among equals. He doesn't need to assert himself or his own opinions on every single issue. He doesn't need to feel that his ideas always need to be implemented, much less that the other elders should "obey" him personally. The authority of the pastor is derived and declarative. In other words, the pastor has authority only insofar as what he is saying is faithful to the message of the one who has sent him.

So even though I am the senior pastor of our church, I do not chair the elders' meetings (or the members' meetings, for that matter). There are even issues that we talk about as elders that I don't weigh in on very noticeably. Sometimes I even abstain on votes! Why? Primarily because I want the nonstaff elders to own the ministry together, but also because I want to protect them from becoming overly dependent on my opinions or from gauging their comments on what they think I'm going to say. I don't want to short-circuit the plurality of our leadership. In fact, I actually want to wean them off of dependence on me as quickly as possible so that they are not inappropriately dependent on paid staff for the leadership of the church. If something were to happen to me, I want them to be able to continue leading the church without missing a step.

Pastoral authority is like soap—the more you use it, the less you have left. What I'm recommending, then, is strong biblical leadership with a light hand. Lead with the Word, through the biblical fidelity of your expositional preaching and the biblical content of the songs you sing together in corporate worship. As the Word is placed front and center, it will begin to shape people without needing you to exercise your authority or weigh in heavily on every decision that's made. Granted, you need to lead, and you can't just be silent on everything. But lead with the Word, not simply with the strength of your personality or opinions.

A special word to senior pastors: it is a special privilege to be the Timothy in Ephesus, the main preaching or teaching pastor (we call it the "senior pastor"). More than anyone else's, my teaching of God's Word shapes the life of the congregation. The ministry of these other elders refines, reflects, and reproduces this main teaching ministry. It doesn't hinder what God calls me to do in this congregation—it helps.

Speaking Graciously

Here are a few things to think about as you consider how to go about leading or participating in elders' meetings.

Humility. "With humility of mind regard one another as more important than yourselves" (Phil. 2:3). This is the first and probably most important rule for cultivating healthy, fruitful elders' meetings. Spiritual and intellectual pride corrodes elderships. Genuine humility is something of a built-in shock absorber—it defuses both the potential offensiveness of some positive ideas and the potential defensiveness that some criticisms might otherwise engender. The absence of humility is often what detonates elders' meetings. Speak and listen with humility.

Biblical warrant. "The unfolding of Your words gives light; it gives understanding to the simple" (Ps. 119:130). As much as possible, have biblical reasons for the things you suggest. Don't just play on the field of logic, personality, or leadership panache. Especially in the early years of an eldership, set the pace and build confidence in your leadership among the other elders by rooting your wisdom in the wisdom of God. You've got to model it yourself before you can expect to see it in others.

Patience. "Reprove, rebuke, exhort, with great patience and instruction" (2 Tim. 4:2). Make haste, but do it slowly. If you're the pastor, then it's likely that you are the one who has been thinking about church organization and structure longer than anyone else in the church. As right as you may very well be, it has taken you a while to get there, hasn't it? God has patiently taught you the elements and forms of healthy church life. Give the congregation and even the other elders time to let things sink in, time to be convinced and own a biblical vision for the church. Go at a pace that enables the congregation to keep up with you. Get used to thinking in terms of years rather than just weeks or months. It'll preserve your pastoral sanity—trust me.

Willingness to yield. "The wisdom from above is first pure, then peaceable, gentle, reasonable, full of mercy and good fruits, unwavering, without hypocrisy. And the seed whose fruit is righteousness is sown in peace by those who make peace. Peacemakers who sow in peace raise a harvest of righteousness" (James 3:17–18). Don't divide the church over matters that are not central to the gospel or to the church's ministry. We have no choice but to stand firm on the deity of Christ, substitutionary atonement, the reality of Christ's attesting miracles, his physical resurrection, and the authority, inspiration, and inerrancy of Scripture. There are also, of course, matters that are not "salvation issues" that are still important for the life of the church. But even on these important yet nonsalvific matters, be willing to yield if it looks as if pressing forward will unnecessarily fracture the church.

Giving and receiving godly encouragement and criticism. This is a skill set that too few pastors have deliberately developed among local church leaders. Improving the mechanics and underpinnings of your church comes only through constructive criticism and encouragement. Provide a periodic time for trusted leaders to give godly, gentle, but forthright feedback on the weekly services, your sermons, the prayers or Scripture readings of other leaders, the business/members' meetings, and even the elders' meetings. Providing that periodic time—whether weekly, twice a month, or monthly—will help sharpen the spiritual senses of your leaders, give them practice at encouraging and sharpening you, and give you practice at receiving godly encouragement and criticism.

Humor. As a pastor, it would be easy to take yourself way too seriously. Resist the temptation! We're just people, and everyone knows it. Even the best of men are men at best. Be quick to laugh at yourself. Be quick to laugh with others. Laughter is one of the best ways to build common rapport, and it keeps both elders' meetings and business meetings appropriately lighthearted, humble, and congenial.

Observing Order

Discussion in an elders' meeting needs to be handled in an orderly way. We've found that the best way to begin discussing a matter is by submitting a one-page memo a week or two before the meeting for all the elders to look at prior to the meeting. This discipline allows each elder to have at least a few days to reflect on the matter before being asked to state his opinion.

A good memo will include a clear proposal or motion for some action to be taken by the elders. This way, when the motion comes to the elder body, it isn't just "I move that we support international missionaries." Rather, it's "I move that we use this line of the budget to support this particular group of international missionaries with this particular amount of money for this particular amount of time." Specific motions are always easier for elders to vote on than ambiguous ones, because the elder body is a deliberative body—it is designed for collaborative decision-making. The clearer the issue the body is asked to decide, the easier it is for the body to make a decision. So before you bring a matter up for discussion, it's wise to be clear in your own mind about what exactly you're asking the elders to decide.

Once the memo is written and distributed, it is put on the agenda for the next elders' meeting. But any motion must be seconded by another elder in order to be discussed. So as the matter comes up for discussion, the moderator or chair of the meeting articulates the specific motion and asks if another elder wants to second the motion. Once the motion is seconded, then the chair asks, "Is there any discussion?" In a smaller elder body, the chair can take a more collegial approach by asking each individual elder for his thoughts. In a larger body, this collegial approach is impractical, so the chair usually alternates between asking the whole group for thoughts for and against the motion, until the chair decides that the discussion has gone back and forth long enough and a decision needs to be made. At this point, the chair simply closes the discussion and takes the vote.

Note well, however, that each elder will differ as to how much discussion he is willing to entertain on various issues. And if you rotate the chair of the meeting (who moderates the discussion), then each chair will have particular issues to which he wants to give more (or less) lengthy discussion. Not every elder will weigh the same issues with the same gravity, so not every chair will facilitate the same discussion in the same way. This is part of the reason that a plurality of elders is so valuable—plurality contributes to balance. But it's also part of the reason that a plurality of elders presumes the patience of the elders. Each must be patient with the others, and each must know when to back down for the good of the group.

Voting

Issues placed before the elders are decided by means of voting. In our church, each elder has one vote, including the senior pastor. In our case, most of our motions are carried by a simple majority because demanding a strict unanimity can silence helpful questions and squelch sincere dissent. Unanimity among our own elders is required only when voting on elder nominations, and even this requirement is not in our church's constitution. It is a simple matter of practical prudence. The senior pastor's vote will naturally garner more respect since he is the one handling the Word the most, but there's no need to formalize or quantify that value—it will find a fair-market value as the other elders learn where the senior pastor is wise and where he needs help.

This is where the rubber meets the road, because it's where the humility of each elder is tested. In almost every elders' meeting, one of the elders will be voted down on a particular issue. I myself have been voted down on more occasions than I can remember! How will you respond when it happens to you, perhaps over and over again? Will you get frustrated and angry? Or will you exercise patience and humility, recognizing and valuing the wisdom of the other elders and wisely accepting their counsel, even though it might rub you the wrong way at first? "Wisdom is with those who receive counsel," but "he who hates reproof is stupid" (Prov. 12:1; 13:10). So hold your expectations with an open hand. Maintain a healthy degree of separation between yourself and your ideas. That makes the experience of getting voted down much less problematic, which in turn helps to prevent unnecessary conflict and preserve unity.

There will inevitably be close votes, like 4–3 or 11–9. In those situations, sometimes the motion carries and it's never brought up for additional discussion. Other times, though, the chair may decide to ask for unanimous agreement to revisit the issue in a month, at which time another vote can be taken in hopes of passing the motion with more agreement. Such situations make elder teams grateful for a wise chairman who can see when the elder team needs more time and when it needs to move on. Of course, you can always agree to demand a supermajority on issues like constitutional changes, doctrinal revisions, or unanimity with the freedom to abstain when a few elders lack sufficient acquaintance with a person or situation in a larger congregation. These are all matters of prudence for elder teams to decide in light of their own local circumstances.

Recommended Reading for Section 4

ON ELDERS' WORK

Dever, Mark. *Understanding Church Leadership* (Nashville: B&H, 2014).

Dickson, David. *The Elder and His Work* (Phillipsburg, NJ: P&R, 2004).

Naselli, Andrew. *Conscience: What It Is, How to Train It, and Loving Those Who Differ* (Wheaton, IL: Crossway, 2016).

Newton, Phil, and Matt Schmucker. *Elders in the Life of the Church: Rediscovering the Biblical Model for Church Leadership* (Grand Rapids, MI: Kregel, 2014).

Piper, John. *Biblical Eldership* (Minneapolis: Desiring God Ministries, 1999).

Rinne, Jeramie. *Church Elders: How to Shepherd God's People Like Jesus* (Wheaton, IL: Crossway, 2014).

Conclusion

SO WHAT IS ALL THIS FOR? I mean, where is all this deliberateness and intentionality going? What's it aimed at? Of course, the goal all along has been a healthy church. But in what does the church's health consist? Certainly it consists in holiness, faith, love, and sound doctrine (Eph. 4:14–16; 1 Thess. 3:12–13; 1 Tim. 1:5; 6:3–4). These must always be our paramount concerns. But the health of the local church is also discerned in the direction of its gaze (2 Cor. 3:18). Whom is your local church looking at?

A Godward-Looking Church

"But we all, with unveiled face, beholding as in a mirror the glory of the Lord, are being transformed into the same image from glory to glory, just as from the Lord, the Spirit" (2 Cor. 3:18; cf. 1 John 3:2). Transformation into the likeness of the Lord happens as we gaze at him together over time. The biblical hallmarks of church health—holiness, faith, love, sound doctrine—are cultivated in us as we are captivated by him.

What this means is that we want to build our churches in a way that makes this corporate captivation with Christ a normal part of our lives together. We want to create opportunities to be captivated together by the beauty of his character and work. At least, that's what it meant for Paul. He goes on to say in 2 Corinthians 4 that as a consequence of receiving this transforming ministry of God's Word, he refuses to distort or add to the Word of God in the way that he carries out his ministry. Rather, he commends the legitimacy of his ministry in God's sight "by setting forth the truth plainly" (2 Cor. 4:2 NIV 1984). This makes perfect sense. If people are transformed ever more perfectly into the image of Christ by gazing at him, then the job of the pastor and evangelist is not to come up with more innovative or clever methods. It is rather to present people with the clearest picture possible of biblical truth. The more clearly we present Christ's person and work to our local churches, the more clearly we will come to reflect his glory together as if in a mirror.

This is why it's so important to begin (and continue!) a work by expositional preaching that clarifies the gospel and makes much of God. This is why we want to present God and Christ clearly and frequently in evangelism. This is why we want to keep all our methods as plain as possible—so that we don't obscure our message with our method. This is also why we want to be careful to use only the forms and elements prescribed by God's Word in our corporate worship gatherings; and it's why we want to be careful that the elders we nominate are not simply men who lead in the community, but are men whose lives have been transformed to reflect the glory of God's holiness, love, and truth. Nothing else has transforming power for the church but the Word of God plainly set forth in preaching and in living.

The recent trend in pastoral ministry has been to come up with increasingly clever and innovative models or metaphors for ministry that still retain some semblance of faithfulness to God's Word. Much of this recent activity has had its genesis in the thinking of the church growth movement. Bigger must be best, so the primary goal has shifted from how to cultivate health to how to get big. Many books in this camp are designed to make the church appeal to the world on the world's terms rather than on God's terms. But this only amounts to so much worldly wisdom (1 Cor. 2:1–5). As our ministry methods become more complex, more reliant on human ingenuity, and more concerned with the approval of the world, they begin to cast a shadow on the image of God, and "the Light of the knowledge of the glory of God in the face of Christ" (2 Cor. 4:6) appears correspondingly dimmer. The mirror of God's Word becomes increasingly opaque, tarnished by the overapplication of human technique, and the result is a gradual diminishing of the transforming power that enables the church to reflect the character and knowledge of God.

It is in this context that we are encouraging churches to become more deliberate about "setting forth the truth plainly." People are transformed and renewed in the likeness of Christ when they look at God as he has revealed himself in both his written and his incarnate Word. The job of the church, then, is not to show people a reflection of themselves. We are instead biblically obliged to raise their gaze, redirecting their attention from themselves to their Creator. There is no secret to a transforming Christian ministry save the power of God's Word and the life-giving breath of his Spirit (Ezek. 37:1–14). You don't need a catchy new metaphor. You don't need the latest evangelism program. You don't need to change the name of your church. You don't need a pastor with a grand scheme for growth, effectiveness, and success as the world would define them. What is needed most today is a commitment to being deliberate about setting forth the truth plainly, because the truth as we gaze on it in Christ is what transforms us, what builds us up and sets us free (John 17:17; Acts 20:32; John 8:36).

So a healthy church is a Godward-looking church. We look in dependence on him for our message, our method, and the transformation of our churches into the image of Christ.

An Outward-Looking Church

As we gaze at God, we notice not only that he is delighting in his own perfections, as we would expect an all-sufficient being to do. We also notice that he is looking outward, looking to bless his people and to draw others in to be a part of his redeemed community, the church. God is satisfied in himself—he does not need us, and he is uppermost in his own affections. Yet God is not exclusively self-absorbed. He wants his gospel to go to the nations, not just remain within certain geopolitical confines. Heaven will be a place where every tribe, tongue, people, and nation will be represented around the throne of God. And this great variety will glorify him all the more.

If we are to be imitators of God (Eph. 5:1), then our churches will reflect something of that same outward-looking focus. Part of being a healthy church means not being satisfied with self-absorption. Yes, we are right to show concern for the purity and corporate testimony of our churches. But being outward looking—looking for opportunities to be a blessing to other individuals, other churches, and other countries—is part of corporate maturity as a church body.

Other individuals. It would be easy to allow ourselves and others to get away with treating the church as if it's designed simply to meet our own needs as spiritual consumers. In one sense, there's nothing wrong at all with coming to church to get our needs met. Christians are not self-sufficient. The Christian life is to be lived out in community. God has met our most fundamental need by forgiving us of our sins when we repented of them and believed in Jesus Christ. We all need distinctively Christian fellowship, and we find a community of believers in the church. We need to hear good preaching, have encouraging conversations, and be challenged in our faith, and there would be something wrong if we were not coming to church precisely in order to meet these spiritual needs.

Yet if we are coming to church only as consumers to have our own needs met, then we have missed the point of the church. We are not merely intended to have our needs met. We are intended to be part of God's plan for drawing other people to himself and for encouraging and building up those who are already his children. Each member is not simply intended to be a consumer. We are all intended to be providers. We are colaborers with God himself in the work of the gospel

(1 Cor. 3:9)! Some of us may well be introverted or less talkative. But none of us are designed merely to be ministered to, as if the whole church revolved around our own felt needs and desires. We are all called to "stimulate one another to love and good deeds" and to "bear one another's burdens" (Heb. 10:24; Gal. 6:2). Wise pastors and church leaders, then, encourage people to take an outward-looking stance toward other members.

Look around at your church. Who's sitting alone? Who has no one to talk with after the service is over and people are milling around? Go talk to that person and be an encouragement to him. Are there older members who could use a ride to church? Offer to pick them up and take them home. Exercise hospitality with singles or newly-wed couples. Budget to take a visitor or new member to lunch once a month. Plan to meet people for lunch during the week to encourage them and build them up in their faith. Read a good Christian book with another believer. Point out evidences of God's grace in other people's lives—even if they're only dim reflections of God's character. Look for an area where the church could use more servants and pitch in, even if it's not necessarily an area where you are particularly gifted to serve. The nursery is almost always a good place to start. Church bodies grow biblically when each individual part is doing its work and contributing proportionally. If you are a member of a local church, then you are part of God's plan for the growth of that church (Eph. 4:11–16).

Other churches. Yet our outward-looking responsibilities don't just stop within the friendly confines of our own church. Churches show corporate maturity when they show loving concern for other local churches in the area. Often we think of an outward focus in either individual or global terms. But part of being a mature local congregation is realizing that there are other solidly evangelical congregations right in our own backyards who may or may not be as far along as ours. If they're not as far along, offer them resources for further theological and practical development—books, booklets, good sermons to listen to, conference scholarships, or simply a corporate cash gift to get a worthy ministry off the ground. We've been on both sides of these kinds of gracious exchanges and can attest to the great encouragement that such gifts from other churches can be. If your church has been enlarged by God's grace and there's a new church plant in an area where a few of your families live, then offer to contribute those families (with their consent, of course!) as a mature addition to the existing core group.

If the church is a peer church, or is further along than your own, then perhaps you could foster a relationship with them and consider how you can point out evidences of grace that will encourage and spur them on to further obedience and faithfulness. Seek to partner with them for the cause of the gospel, and if they are more theologically mature, seek to expose yourself and the church you serve to the teaching and modeling of their leaders.

One of the ways we've tried to encourage other churches is by hosting an internship program for aspiring pastors. This internship has proven to be an invaluable learning experience for the young men who have completed it, and their churches will be benefited by the time, teaching, and resources we pour into them while they're here.

Another way we've tried to encourage other churches is by hosting 9Marks Weekenders. These are quarterly opportunities to spend a long weekend taking a look behind the scenes of a healthy church. Participants get to sit in on an elders' meeting, hear a talk on expositional preaching, learn how our church went from being unhealthy to being thriving and vibrant, hear me (Mark) talk about how I prepare sermons and plan Sunday morning services, see how we take in new members through the new members' class—and then they get to see it all come together during the Sunday morning and Sunday evening services.

There are all sorts of ways that local churches can help one another. If God decides to bless your church with spiritual maturity and numerical growth, work among your own congregation to cultivate a culture in which helping other churches is a priority. It is simply a good thing for healthy churches to offer other pastors and church leaders opportunities to see such healthy church practices modeled in real life.

Other countries. But even after we've helped other local churches, we still haven't approximated the scope of God's heart. His outward look is global. He wants the righteousness and praise of his people to spring up before all nations (Isa. 61:11). He is, even now, raising up his banner to all the peoples (49:22), and he is doing it by sending the likes of us to make disciples of all nations (Matt. 28:18–20). The present reality that fills heaven is the praise of every tribe, tongue, people, and nation (Rev. 7:9–10), and the destiny of God's churches is conformity to the image of Christ and eternal unity with the diverse multitude of heaven (Rom. 8:29; 1 John 3:2).

God is calling us to keep this destiny in mind as we seek to build up his churches. He is seeking worshipers for himself who will worship him in Spirit and in truth (John 4:21–24), and all history is moving irresistibly forward, toward the final day when the whole earth will be harvested by God's angels and the wheat will be separated from the weeds (Matt. 13:24–43). God intends the life of the church to be an evangelistic display of God's glory to unbelieving communities, and a powerful evidence of the wisdom of his inaugurated reign to the heavenly powers and authorities (1 Pet. 2:9–12; Eph. 3:10–11). The local church is *the* major player, under God's providence, in the accomplishment of God's purposes in human history, and his ultimate vision for the church actually surpasses even the global stage. God intends our influence by his Spirit to have literally cosmic implications—and the biblical form of the church is designed specifically to accommodate the function God intends it to fulfill.

As we go about building up God's church, then, it is incumbent upon us as leaders to ensure that the local church we serve is an outward-looking church, aware of the global and even cosmic agenda God has set for us. We're not advocating church planting on Neptune! Rather, we should be cultivating among our congregations a deep concern for the fame of God's name to extend to other parts of the globe through the preaching of his gospel to all the nations, and for the corporate testimony of our own local church to function as a manifestation of God's wisdom and power to the authorities that hold sway under his sovereignty in the spiritual realm.

These are the things we need to be praying specifically about as churches. These are the things that we should be strategizing for, whether in elders' meetings or coffee shops. These are the things we should be planning and budgeting for. We need to be teaching people that a biblical church is about much more than simply meeting our felt needs for purpose, significance, fellowship, and mutual understanding. It is about the glory of God in the gospel of Christ. We need to be weaning members off the expectation of being served or even entertained, and training them rather to expect to become a contributing part of a global and even cosmic corporate cause to glorify God among the nations and in the heavenly halls of power.

As the elder ultimately responsible for the teaching and leadership of the church, the senior pastor should be the primary champion of the missions cause in the local church where he serves. Too often it happens that the pastor is the one who is arguing for more money and resources to be devoted to programs that serve only the members of the local church. This pastoral mentality often leaves other church leaders in the awkward position of trying to convince the pastor to increase the percentage of the budget devoted both to domestic and foreign missions.

If you are a pastor, let me challenge you to work toward increasing the percentage of your budget devoted to missions by 1 or 2 percent each year for the next ten years. It's an appropriate strategy, considering the purpose of the church, and it shows other leaders that you are more concerned about the glory of God than you are about your salary and benefits, or about the comfort of particular members. Depending on the size of your budget and the current faithfulness of member giving, it can be a significant step of faith. Above all, it simply honors God to invest his resources for the international expansion of his fame.

The message of this book isn't about flow charts and outlines. It's not about fresh metaphors or new growth graphs. It's about a vision of a whole church deliberately ordered and led so as to facilitate its own edification and ministry. Careful time management allows for more spontaneity and free time; careful budgeting allows for more discretionary income. In the same way, carefully planned church order and leadership frees the church to become the holy and winsome display of God's glory that God himself designed it to be. This book is designed to help liberate both leaders and members from the tyranny of popular growth models and church fads. Imagine—freedom from the tyranny of the new; freedom to become a body of believers in which membership really matters; freedom to become a church that is an increasingly clear display of God's wisdom and glory to the heavenly powers and to the surrounding community. Imagine!

Appendix

Church Membership Interview Form

Date: ________________

Staff Attending Interview

Pastor: ____________________

Other Staff/Guest: _________________ ______________________

Applicant Information

Name: ____________________________ Birth date: ____________

Address: ____

Home Phone: _________________ Cell Phone: _________________

Occupation: ____

Work Phone: __________________ Email: ____________________

Married: _____ Yes _____ No Wedding date: _____________

Children

Name 1: _______________ birth date: ____________ notes:

Name 2: _______________ birth date: ____________ notes:

Name 3: _______________ birth date: ____________ notes:

Name 4: ________________ birth date: _____________ notes:

Name 5: ________________ birth date: _____________ notes:

Name 6: ________________ birth date: _____________ notes:

Previous Church Membership: _________________________________

Baptized (date/location): ______________________________________

How Introduced to Our Church? ______________________________

Began Attending: __________

Membership Class (date): __________

Comments?

Membership by:

Baptism (date) ______________ Statement ________ Letter ________

Sent to: ________________________________ Received: ____________

Other Family Information:

Divorced: _____ Yes _____ No Notes: _____________________

Personal Background / Experience:

Interested in a Small-Group Bible Study?

Men _____ Women _____ Married _____ Mixed _____

Interested in 1-1 Discipleship? _____ Yes _____No

Wednesday Evening Service

Comments?

Sunday Evening Service

Comments?

Sunday Morning Service

Comments?

Nine Marks Booklet _____ Yes _____ No

Comments?

Prior Church Discipline _____ Yes _____ No

If Yes, Why?

Sign Church Covenant _____ Yes _____ No

Comments?

Sign Statement of Faith _____ Yes _____ No

Comments?

Understands Gospel _____ Yes _____ No

Comments?

Recommended: _____ Yes _____ No

Date: ________________________

Notes

Mark's Preface

1. Mark Dever, *Nine Marks of a Healthy Church* (Wheaton, IL: Crossway, 2004, 2000; original edition, Cape Coral, FL: Founders Press, 1997).
2. Mark Dever, ed., *Polity: Biblical Arguments on How to Conduct Church Life* (Washington, DC: Center for Church Reform, 2001).
3. Mark Dever, *Understanding Church Leadership* (Nashville: B&H, 2016).
4. Mark Dever, *The Church: The Gospel Made Visible* (Nashville: B&H Academic, 2012).

Paul's Preface

1. To sign up for a 9Marks Weekender, visit www.9marks.org, hit the "Events" tab, and scroll to "Weekenders."

A Note to the Reader

1. "Now I commit you to God and to the word of his grace, which can build you up and give you an inheritance among all those who are sanctified" (Acts 20:32 NIV 1984).
2. Luke 11:13; Eph. 1:17; 3:16; Rev. 3:1. See Iain Murray, *Pentecost—Today?* (Cape Coral, FL: Founders Press, 1998), 20–21.
3. John 6:44; Acts 11:18; 1 Cor. 2:14–16; 3:7; Eph. 2:8–9; 2 Pet. 1:1.

Introduction

1. Rick Warren, *The Purpose Driven Church* (Grand Rapids, MI: Zondervan, 1995).
2. James White, *Rethinking the Church* (Grand Rapids, MI: Baker, 2003).
3. Dan Kimball, *The Emerging Church* (Grand Rapids, MI: Zondervan, 2003).
4. Wolfgang Simson, *Houses That Change the World* (Carlisle, Cumbria, UK: Paternoster, 2001).
5. This is not to claim we have proof texts for all our practices. The new member interview is not found in the Bible. Yet it is a methodological expression of our understanding of the content and primacy of the gospel, and the importance of the purity of the membership of the local church and her gospel witness in the surrounding community.

Chapter 1: The Four P's

1. Throughout the rest of the book, first-person pronouns with reference to the authors refer to Mark Dever, not Paul Alexander.
2. For a simple scriptural defense of the interchangeability of the expressions "the gospel" and "God's word," see Paul's interchangeable use of the terms in 1 Thessalonians 2:9, 13. He says in 2:9 that what he "proclaimed" to them was "the gospel of God"; yet in verse 13 he says that what they "received" and "heard" from him was "the word of God."
3. For more on how to preach the content and intent of a Scripture passage, see John Stott, *Between Two Worlds* (Grand Rapids, MI: Eerdmans, 1982), or David Helm, *Expositional Preaching: How We Speak God's Word Today* (Wheaton, IL: Crossway, 2014). On how to plan both sermons and services, see the *9Marks Journal* on "Expositional Preaching" at www.9marks.org/journal/expositional-preaching/.
4. Cf. D. A. Carson, *A Call to Spiritual Reformation: Priorities from Paul and His Prayers* (Grand Rapids, MI: Baker, 1992).
5. "Four Decades of Ministry with John MacArthur," recorded July 12, 2002. The interview is available for online listening and download at www.9marks.org/interview/four-decades-ministry-john-macarthur/.

Chapter 2: Beginning the Work

1. For help in learning how to preach the gospel from any biblical passage, see Graeme Goldsworthy, *Preaching the Whole Bible as Christian Scripture* (Grand Rapids, MI: Eerdmans, 2000). For a more rigorous treatment of preaching the gospel from the Old Testament particularly, see Sidney Greidanus, *Preaching Christ from the Old Testament* (Grand Rapids, MI: Eerdmans, 1999). See also Bryan Chappell's helpful textbook *Christ-Centered Preaching* (Grand Rapids, MI: Baker, 1994).
2. Fuller biblical arguments for local church membership can be found in Mark Dever, *Nine Marks of a Healthy Church* (Wheaton, IL: Crossway, 2000) or Dever's booklet *A Display of God's Glory* (Washington, DC: 9Marks Ministries, 2001). The how-to's of removing members will be discussed in chap. 5.
3. I did not publicly describe these meetings as "reverse membership interviews." I simply visited with current members in their homes, listening to their perceptions of previous pastors, of church difficulties, and of what was going well in the church. In doing this, I was listening for, and in most cases asking for, a quick explanation of the gospel.

Chapter 3: Doing Responsible Evangelism

1. See Colin Marshall and Tony Payne, *The Trellis and the Vine* (Kingsford, Australia: Matthias Media, 2009).

Chapter 4: Taking in New Members

1. For a fuller treatment, see Mark Dever, *A Display of God's Glory: Deacons, Elders, Congregationalism, and Membership* (Washington, DC: 9Marks Ministries, 2001).

2. The manuscripts for each talk are available for free download and unrestricted copying and use at https://www.capitolhillbaptist.org/resources/core-seminars /series/membership-matters/.
3. It is often argued that the downside to delaying a person's membership or baptism just to fit them into a new members' class is that you're denying them fellowship, or even a means of grace, for what seems to be administrative trivia. But Paul's wisdom to Timothy concerning elder nominations is just as true for member nominations and baptismal candidates: "Do not lay hands upon anyone too hastily and thereby share responsibility for the sins of others; keep yourself free from sin" (1 Tim. 5:22). It is better to allow the behavior of potential members to either confirm or deny their verbal profession *before* they become part of the corporate testimony of the church rather than after. Many evangelical churches have failed to understand that patience is a virtue in taking in new members.

Chapter 5: Doing Church Discipline

1. This, of course, assumes the use of a formal set of guidelines for deliberative meetings, such as *Robert's Rules of Order.*

Chapter 6: Understanding the Regulative Principle

1. On the regulative principle, see Philip Graham Ryken, Derek W. H. Thomas, and J. Ligon Duncan III, eds., *Give Praise to God: A Vision for Reforming Worship* (Phillipsburg, NJ: Presbyterian & Reformed, 2003), 17–73. For a historical introduction, see Iain Murray, *The Reformation of the Church: A Collection of Reformed and Puritan Documents on Church Issues* (Carlisle, PA: Banner of Truth, 1965), 35–58.
2. D. A. Carson, ed., *Worship by the Book* (Grand Rapids, MI: Zondervan, 2002), 55, emphasis original.
3. Carson, *Worship by the Book*, 55.
4. See J. Ligon Duncan III, "Does God Care How We Worship?" and "Foundations for Biblically Directed Worship," in Ryken, Thomas, and Duncan, eds., *Give Praise to God*, 17–73.
5. See also Lev. 10:1–3 (ESV), where God kills Nadab and Abihu for bringing "unauthorized fire" before him; or 1 Chron. 13:7–11, where God kills Uzzah for touching the ark to keep it from falling off a cart that God had not authorized for its transportation (Ex. 25:14; 1 Chron. 15:13).
6. See Duncan, "Does God Care How We Worship?" in Ryken, Thomas, and Duncan, eds., *Give Praise to God*, 43.

Chapter 7: Applying the Regulative Principle

1. The following assumes that the purpose of the Sunday morning gathering is primarily edification and secondarily evangelism. See chap. 10 for a brief defense of prioritizing edification on Sunday mornings.
2. J. Ligon Duncan III, "Foundations for Biblically Directed Worship," in Philip Graham Ryken, Derek W. H. Thomas, and J. Ligon Duncan III, eds., *Give Praise to God: A Vision for Reforming Worship* (Phillipsburg, NJ: Presbyterian & Reformed, 2003), 65.

3. Before trying to figure out what distinguishes your church from other local churches, you must establish what distinguishes your church from the world. Being formed and reformed according to God's Word is the only answer that will do, because it is the acceptance and application of God's Word, especially as encapsulated in the gospel, that has always marked out the people of God from the world (Gen. 12:1–3; Ex. 19:5–6; Deut. 12:29–32; esp. John 17:14; Eph. 4:17–24).
4. E.g., the Nicene Creed of AD 325, its more common form of 381, or the Belgic Confession of 1561. The corporate reading of historic Christian creeds reminds us that we do not confess Christ in a historical vacuum, and it helps prevent us from falling into the chronological snobbery of thinking that we're better because we live later in history.
5. The prayer of confession is best followed by an assurance of pardon read directly from Scripture so that people are not left mourning their sins, but rejoicing in God's merciful forgiveness of them.
6. On praying from Paul's prayers, see Carson, *A Call to Spiritual Reformation*.
7. You might consider having elders or other church leaders pray any of these prayers except the pastoral prayer. Having other elders pray publicly serves to train them in public spiritual leadership, to establish their authority in the eyes of the congregation, and to give the church a more secure sense of being shepherded by a plurality of godly leaders who balance the pastor's weaknesses.
8. You might also consider having some of these prayers prepared beforehand. Far from being "canned," prepared prayers can more intentionally model biblical faithfulness and richness in prayer, and can also help avoid the common public embarrassments of unintentionally long pauses, repetition, or slips of the tongue. Preparation for public prayer does not quench the Holy Spirit, especially if that preparation has been Word centered, because the Holy Spirit blesses and applies the articulation of the Word, not simply spontaneity.
9. The resources I've found most helpful are *The Baptist Hymnal* (Nashville: Convention Press, 1991); *Songs of Fellowship* (Eastbourne, E. Sussex, UK: Kingsway Music, 1995); *Maranatha Praise* (Maranatha! Music, 1993); *Grace Hymns* (London: Grace Publications Trust, 1984); and *Hymns II* (Downers Grove, IL: InterVarsity Press, 1976). I also regularly use *Psalms, Hymns, and Spiritual Songs* (Cape Coral, FL: Founders Press, 1994).
10. This is why the idea of incorporating drama into worship gatherings is actually unnecessary and almost unbiblical. Jesus has instituted his own dramatic presentations of the gospel (Matt. 28:19–20; Luke 22:14–20; Acts 2:38–39; 1 Cor. 11:23–26; Col. 2:11–12). In doing so, is he encouraging us to come up with our own dramatic presentations or to avail ourselves of the ones he's already so graciously ordained?
11. See Acts 19:32, 39, 41, where *ekklēsia* is translated as "assembly."
12. Even if *homothumadon* is translated "with one accord" in Acts 2:46 and 5:12, the weight of the argument rests on the presence of "all" the believers in each particular gathering. It would also be difficult to imagine that all the believers were in "one

accord" if they were refusing or simply neglecting to meet together with the rest of the group at the appointed times.

13. The difficulties here are understood: Does the church cease to be the church if just one member is absent from the gathering? Are denominational divides preventing true church gatherings? Is it wrong to have multiple church gatherings in one city? The questions could be multiplied. The point, though, is that if we covenant as church members to live the Christian life together, yet "congregate" separately (!) in such a way that we never see the other two-thirds of the "congregation," then in what sense are we living the Christian life "together"? In what sense are the multiple gatherings reflecting the corporate unity of the local church?

Chapter 8: The Role of the Pastor

1. See Introduction.
2. For a more detailed treatment of the pastor as practitioner of the marks of a true church, see Mark Dever, "The Noble Task," in *Polity: Biblical Arguments on How to Conduct Church Life* (Washington, DC: 9Marks Ministries, 2001).
3. Criteria for choosing appropriate music for corporate worship will be discussed in chap. 13.
4. The best way to accomplish both objectives in the same sermon is to preach evangelistic, expository messages—sermons that take the point of the passage as the point of the message *and* which clearly present the gospel as the natural outworking of reading every passage through a gospel lens (Luke 24:25–27, 45–47).
5. This is why a church looking for a pastor should not be enamored with an effervescent personality or innovative program that a pastor might bring, but should rather examine his ability to feed the congregation on the milk and meat of the Word. Previous churches in a man's ministry should always be consulted. His preaching (backed by his character) is what will either drive the church forward or drive it into the ground. Struggling churches will not be renewed by embracing another innovative program. They will be renewed by the faithful preaching of the gospel.

Chapter 9: Evangelistic Exposition

1. William Perkins, *The Art of Prophesying* (Edinburgh: Banner of Truth, 1996), 62.
2. For a template of the "Application Grid" that Mark uses when preparing sermons, see https://simeontrust.org/application-grid-9marks/.

Chapter 10: The Roles of the Different Gatherings

1. See especially verses 3, 4, 5, 6, 12, 17, and 26. We also need to be reminded that our audience in worship is God, not men.
2. For a brief explanation of what each of these activities entails, see chap. 7.
3. This could take the form of either raising people's names for prayer and consideration (what we might refer to as putting them on a "care list" of people whose membership might be in jeopardy because of their behavior) or voting to remove a member from the rolls for nonattendance or unrepented sin.

   In a congregational polity, the whole congregation has final authority in matters of personal dispute, discipline, doctrine, and membership (see Matt. 18:15–17;

1 Cor. 5:1–13; Gal. 1:6–9; 2 Cor. 2:6, respectively). As such, final corporate decisions on these matters should be brought before the congregation. For a more complete argument, see Mark Dever, *A Display of God's Glory* (Washington, DC: 9Marks Ministries, 2001).

Chapter 11: The Role of the Ordinances

1. The symbolic play between physical baptism and our spiritual death and resurrection with Christ in Romans 6 and the parallel between physical baptism and *spiritual* circumcision (not physical circumcision) in Colossians 2:11–12 are the main biblical reasons that correlating New Testament baptism with Old Testament circumcision does not work to justify infant baptism.
2. This is certainly not to deny the possibility of genuine conversions during childhood; we *pray* for early conversions! It is simply to question whether or not we can adequately discern in young children the kind of fruit that we are told to look for in order to ascertain the genuineness of a Christian profession.
3. Since baptism and church membership are nonsaving means of grace, withholding them from a minor for a time cannot endanger the soul of the child. Even in the rare case where the soft consciences of young believers may be pricked because they think they are disobeying Christ's command, we understand the delay to be a prudential case of waiting to see them bring forth fruit that gives evidence of repentance in a context disassociated from parental influence.
4. This action communicates either that the leaders of the church are no longer in a position (due to a member's nonattendance) to observe good fruit that evidences repentance or that the leaders are seeing bad fruit that actually contradicts the member's profession of faith and scandalizes the church's corporate testimony.
5. When this happens, the church should also take the member's name off the membership rolls. Yet none of this is to say that a member who is barred from the table and removed from the rolls cannot be reinstated upon evident repentance. Nor is it to say that the disciplined member is unwelcome to attend services. The whole purpose of discipline is to encourage the disciplined individual, through this serious and negative sanction, to repent. It is simply to say that such people are *precluded* from claiming unity with the church by taking the Lord's Supper, and they are *protected* from eating and drinking judgment to themselves (1 Cor. 11:29), because their behavior has not proven the genuineness of their verbal profession of faith.

Chapter 13: Music

1. God told Moses just before the exodus that the Hebrews would worship God at Mount Sinai; and when they got there, they heard his Word.
2. David Peterson, *Engaging with God: A Biblical Theology of Worship* (Downers Grove, IL: InterVarsity Press, 1992), 20.
3. Some appeal to 1 Cor. 14:23 as a biblical reason for calibrating the music in our corporate services to the preferences of unbelieving seekers. But the primary purpose for the main worship gathering in 1 Cor. 14 is edification of believers, not evangelism (see vv. 3, 4, 5, 12, 17, and esp. 25–26: "When you assemble, . . . let all

things be done for edification"). Cf. Heb. 10:24–25. There is still room for evangelism in corporate worship, and even in musical worship. Our point is simply that evangelism is not *primary* in this context. What we need most are seeker-sensitive lives, not seeker-sensitive services.

4. This observation was suggested to me by an insightful self-published booklet by Brian Janssen, *Sing to the Lord a New (Covenant) Song: Thinking about the Songs We Sing to God* (Hospers, IA: Self-published, 2002); available through janssenb@nethtc.net.
5. For a biblical theology of worship, see Carson *Worship by the Book*; Philip Graham Ryken, Derek W. H. Thomas, and J. Ligon Duncan III, eds., *Give Praise to God: A Vision for Reforming Worship* (Phillipsburg, NJ: P&R, 2003); and especially Peterson, *Engaging with God.*
6. We close our eyes for corporate prayer, too, but this is an act of reverence as we bow our heads, not an effort to forget about the people around us.
7. Benjamin Russell Hanby (1833–1867), "Who Is He in Yonder Stall?" quoted from *The Baptist Hymnal* (Nashville: Convention Press, 1991), 124.
8. Many of the Psalms are written in the first-person singular, so we certainly affirm its use in devotional worship. We're simply attempting to address the frequent absence of the corporate aspect of worship in many church worship gatherings.
9. I use the word *confessional* here not in the sense of confessing our sins, but of confessing our common faith in Christian doctrine and our common endeavor in Christian godliness.
10. There is, though, a difference between meditative and manipulative music. Choose wisely. Swooning melodies or overly emotional renditions are equally inappropriate.
11. For examples of such singing today, check out the musical albums from the singing at Together for the Gospel. You can find them at www.t4g.org under "Resources."
12. See Carl Trueman, "What Should Miserable Christians Sing?" *Themelios* 25, no. 2: 2–4.

Chapter 14: The Importance of Elders

1. For a fuller biblical argument for elder leadership in the context of congregational government, see Mark Dever, *Understanding Church Leadership* (Nashville: B&H, 2012); Jeramie Rinne, *Church Elders: How to Shepherd God's People Like Jesus* (Wheaton, IL: Crossway, 2014); and Phil Newton and Matt Schmucker, *Elders in the Life of the Church: Rediscovering the Biblical Model for Church Leadership* (Grand Rapids, MI: Kregel, 2014). For historic Baptist arguments on the same topic, see Mark Dever, ed., *Polity: Biblical Arguments on How to Conduct Church Life* (Washington, DC: 9Marks Ministries, 2001).
2. Note the same interchangeability of "elders" (*presbuterous*) and "the overseer" (*episkopon*) in Titus 1:5–7.
3. Cf. Acts 14:23, where Paul and Barnabas appoint elders (*presbuterous*, plural) in every church (*kat' ekklesian*, distributive singular).
4. Cf. Titus 1:9.

5. For an excellent practical guide on how to lead in this change, see Newton and Schmucker, *Elders in the Life of the Church*.
6. Here we will make the argument without reference to the multiple-deacon aspect of the issue. For that, see Mark Dever, *A Display of God's Glory* (Washington, DC: 9Marks Ministries, 2001).

Chapter 15: Looking for a Few Good Men

1. This section presumes that every ruling elder is a teaching elder; that is, that there is no such distinction intended in 1 Tim. 5, and that the very essence of the office of elder is teaching. If you are in a church that distinguishes these two duties as separate offices, that distinction would certainly affect the training process.
2. E.g., being a lover of money, being argumentative, not being gentle, not managing his own household well (1 Tim. 3:1–7).
3. For a discussion of gender roles in current evangelical church life, see the *9Marks Journal*, "Complementarianism: A Moment of Reckoning," December 2019. For a specific treatment of 1 Timothy 2:9–15, see Andreas Köstenberger, Thomas Schreiner, and H. Scott Baldwin, eds., *Women in the Church: A Fresh Analysis of 1 Timothy 2:9–15* (Grand Rapids, MI: Baker, 1995).
4. This is distinguished from the office of deacon, which is designed for the service of the church through tending to the physical and financial matters of the corporate body.
5. We will think more carefully about what it means to be "able to teach" in chap. 16, and the practical necessity of godly character in chap. 17.

Chapter 16: Assessment

1. It should be understood that no one will meet these criteria perfectly. But these are the questions you want to be asking, and these are the qualities you want to be looking for. In chap. 17, we'll see why the work of the elder requires a growing measure of all these character traits.
2. It might be wise to hold an informal "service review" on Sunday evenings. This time provides a context for giving and receiving godly constructive criticism and encouragement for those who have helped teach or lead in the adult education hour or the Sunday morning or evening services. You might consider inviting the teachers and elders who observed them to your home on Sunday evenings to do this. This kind of constructive criticism can also be given in one-on-one discipling lunches during the week. We implemented a "Service Review" time on Sunday evenings to the great improvement of nonstaff teachers as well as potential elders, and consequently to the tremendous profit of the church.
3. In asking for the opinions of others, we would avoid publicly referring to such questions as "surveys," simply because doing so may encourage less mature members to treat the results as a democratic mandate.

Chapter 18: Getting Started

1. Again, on this point we highly recommend Phil Newton and Matt Schmucker, *Elders in the Life of the Church: Rediscovering the Biblical Model for Church Leadership* (Grand Rapids, MI: Kregel, 2014).

2. This need for biblical instruction is the reason that it is so difficult to work for reform in a church without either being the pastor or having a pastor already committed to expositional preaching and biblical church governance. The pulpit is the primary instrument of change, in terms of both timing and logic. Without biblical instruction, change in the local church is a hard sell—and usually should be!
3. The objection may be raised that preaching on elders is to no purpose for the congregation if the pastor is primarily the one tasked with recognition and nomination. But the congregation must be biblically informed enough to agree that the elder-led form of congregationalism is biblical, to discern who among them might be worthy of recommendation for the pastor's consideration, to discern who might not be so worthy, and to either affirm or deny the pastor's nominations based on the character and ability qualifications outlined in 1 Timothy 3:1–7 and Titus 1:6–9.
4. It may also be wise to give each nominee the opportunity to share his testimony at a normally well-attended public meeting of the church. This will introduce the nominee to newer members and may help more skeptical members become more comfortable with his character and personality.

Chapter 19: Staffing

1. Cf. John Piper, *Brothers, We Are* Not *Professionals* (Nashville: Broadman & Holman, 2002).
2. Single guys cost less to maintain; an undergraduate degree proves personal responsibility; and it's good to catch them before they go to seminary so they don't waste the time and money if they prove unfit for ministry. This way you teach them that the ultimate training ground for pastoral ministry is the local church, not the seminary, and you can actually provide them with a confident sense of being sent to seminary and then into ministry by a whole local church that affirms their pastoral gifting and calling, and that can hopefully provide a measure of financial support as well.
3. For more on deacons, their biblical qualifications, and their relationship to church staff and elders, see Matt Smethurst, *Deacons: How They Serve and Strengthen the Church* (Wheaton, IL: Crossway, 2021).
4. For more on these relationships, see my booklet *Understanding Church Leadership* (Nashville: B&H, 2012).

Chapter 21: The Agenda: What to Talk About

1. Members who are unable to attend because of physical disability, schooling, or military deployment are obviously excepted and are put in the section of the directory entitled "Members in the Area but Unable to Attend," or "Members out of the Area."
2. If you're a pastor or church leader, you are welcome to come and observe one of our elders' meetings. Log onto www.9marks.org, go to the "Events" tab, and scroll down to sign up for the next 9Marks Weekender.
3. If you don't have any of these men, pray that God would send you some or develop the men already in the church!

General Index

Scripture Index

IX 9Marks

Building Healthy Churches

9Marks exists to equip church leaders with a biblical vision and practical resources for displaying God's glory to the nations through healthy churches.

To that end, we want to see churches characterized by these nine marks of health:

1. Expositional Preaching
2. Gospel Doctrine
3. A Biblical Understanding of Conversion and Evangelism
4. Biblical Church Membership
5. Biblical Church Discipline
6. A Biblical Concern for Discipleship and Growth
7. Biblical Church Leadership
8. A Biblical Understanding of the Practice of Prayer
9. A Biblical Understanding and Practice of Missions

More Resources from 9Marks

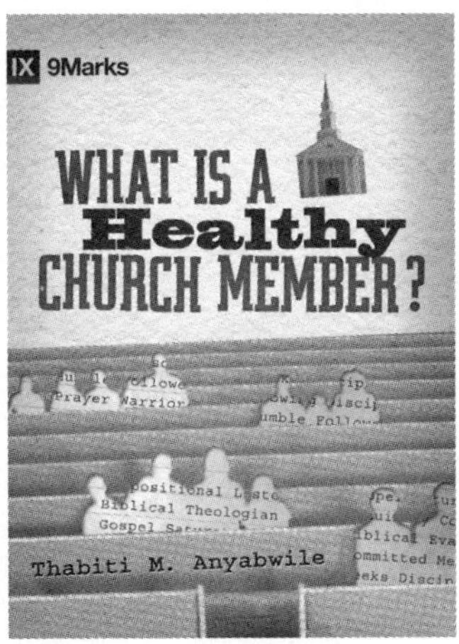

For more information, visit **crossway.org**.